Wintering
Into
Wisdom

Dr. Betty Lentz Siegel
Kennesaw State University President 1981–2006

Wintering

Into

Wisdom

A Festschrift for Dr. Betty Lentz Siegel
Kennesaw State University President 1981-2006

Edited by Elizabeth Giddens

**Kennesaw State
University Press**

Kennesaw State University Press
Kennesaw State University
Building 27, Suite 220, Mailbox 2701
1000 Chastain Road
Kennesaw, GA 30144

Daniel S. Papp, President of the University
Lendley C. Black, Provost & Vice President for Academic Affairs
Laura S. Dabundo, Director of the Press
Shirley Parker Cordell, Senior Administrative Specialist
Sarah L. Johnson, Promotion and Marketing Manager

Elizabeth Giddens, Editor
Jennifer Clifton, Cathleen Salsburg, and Melissa Stiers, Editorial Assistants
Michelle R. Hinson, Production Editor & Book Design
Holly S. Miller, Cover Design
Mimi Fittipaldi, Cover Photo

Library of Congress Cataloging-in-Publication Data

Wintering into wisdom: a festschrift for Dr. Betty Lentz Siegel, Kennesaw State University president, 1981-2006 / edited by Elizabeth Giddens.
    p. cm.
  Includes bibliographical references.
  ISBN 978-1-933483-14-6
  1. Education, Higher. 2. College teachers--Conduct of life. I. Giddens, Elizabeth. II. Siegel, Betty L.
  LB2325.W54 2008
  378--dc22

                              2007035036

Printed in the United States of America
10 9 8 7 6 5 4 3 2 1

Acknowledgments

I am grateful to many Kennesaw State University faculty and staff for their assistance with this volume. Dr. Barbara Stevenson, interim chair of the English Department from 2005 to 2006, first suggested the idea to Dr. Laura Dabundo, director of the Kennesaw Press. Dr. Dabundo, in turn, quickly recognized the import of the project. Her enthusiasm and support for it have made it a reality. Lynda K. Johnson, Betty Siegel's executive assistant, played a key role in identifying and contacting contributors to the volume. Dr. Michael Tierce, associate professor of English, and Dr. Craig Watson, Dr. Siegel's long-time collaborator and speechwriter, also helped guide the development of the book's contents. I am particularly grateful to Dr. Watson for providing me with copies of publications from his personal archive, for assistance in confirming a number of details and facts, and for his excellent suggestions throughout.

The staff of the KSU Press has been wonderful to work with and made the editing process both enjoyable and personally rewarding. Shirley Parker Cordell helped with contracts and correspondence. Holly Miller provided an appealing book cover, and Michelle Hinson provided the book design, which she also skillfully executed as production editor. Sarah L. Johnson has shown insight and skill in positioning this book so that it may reach those readers engaged in the study of leadership and of higher education administration. Special thanks go to Melissa Stiers and Cathleen Salsburg who worked tirelessly over two semesters to track down references and to assist in editing the manuscript. How I respect their sharp eyes and well-tuned ears.

I am indebted to the volume's contributors for the quality and resonance of their essays. They all were enthusiastic about participating in this project, and I appreciate their willingness to devote time from their demanding schedules to join in the effort.

And, finally, I am grateful to Dr. Siegel for her years of service to the university and to the community. She has indeed touched us all.

Elizabeth Giddens
July 2007

Contents

Introduction

"So learn from this
and understand true values. I who tell you
have wintered into wisdom."
Beowulf 1722-24

*T*he title of this volume was suggested by the leader and scholar whom it honors, Dr. Betty Siegel. She had the title on the tip of her tongue, it seemed, when Dr. Laura Dabundo, Director of the Kennesaw State University Press, Dr. Barbara Stevenson, Interim English Department Chair, and I first met with her to propose this festschrift, which celebrates her 25 years as president of Kennesaw College and, subsequently, Kennesaw State University (KSU). President Siegel suggested the phrase, and the three of us instantly liked it for its imagery and suitability. Nothing much more was said about the meaning of the title that day in the winter of 2006; we simply accepted it as the perfect note to sound on the occasion of recognizing the many achievements of one of the longest serving women presidents of a public institution of higher education.

Notably, the phrase "wintering into wisdom," is adapted from a line in *Beowulf*, that 12th-century epic poem about the warrior-hero who slays monsters and frees oppressed people. But the two sentences that constitute the complete thought expressed by the phrase are not spoken by the poem's protagonist; instead they are uttered by Hrothgar, king of the Danes, as he thanks Beowulf in the great hall after the hero's triumph over Grendel. They are words of advice that follow the king's praise for Beowulf's service to the Danes as well as, curiously, an anecdote about some other successful warrior, Heremod, who, in short, "brought little joy/ to the Danish people, only death and destruction" (1711-12). Apparently, Heremod's virtue was undone by his ego; despite the fact that fate had marked him for success: "He suffered in the end / for having plagued his people for so long:/ His life lost happiness" (1720-22). In contrast to Heremod, Hrothgar advises Beowulf to do what his predecessor did not, remain "your people's mainstay and your own warriors'/ helping hand" (1708-09).

The suitability of this volume's title became more and more evident as each contributor submitted his or her essay for the book. Each brown envelope containing new dates and details, new anecdotes and favorite quotations highlighted a facet of Dr. Siegel's career to paint, as a group, a full portrait of the person and the leader, and, more broadly, to establish a communal ethos among those who have been a part of the culture Dr. Siegel has fostered at KSU and beyond. Not only does Dr. Siegel find a fitting parallel in the wise Danish King by serving as Kennesaw State University's president for twenty-five years and nurturing its growth from a four-year college with 4,000 students and 15 baccalaureate programs to university status with more than 18,000 and 55 undergraduate and graduate programs. But there is also a similarity to the poem's hero since Dr. Siegel has been one of those leaders who understands true values and became the mainstay of KSU's students, staff, faculty, and community during her term from 1981 to 2006. The essays testify to key qualities of Dr. Siegel such as her enthusiasm for life, for colleagues, and for work; her persistence to reach goals; her appreciation of the need for balance between the personal and professional aspects of a productive career; and her recognition that everyone of every rank and station needs to find such a balance and needs the consideration of colleagues in the work of achieving that balance in order for individuals as well as the institution as a whole to thrive.

Her positive frame of mind and her respectful empathy for others led to Dr. Siegel's major achievements and, if you think about it, characterize them as well. During her long tenure as KSU's president, and, by the way, as the first woman to head an institution in the 35-unit University System of George, Dr. Siegel founded exemplary programs in minority recruitment, leadership, study-abroad, and student support, including an award-winning honors program, long standing Freshman/Senior-Year Experience Programs, a Sophomore Experience Program, and a recently recognized learning communities initiative. All of these achievements stem from an awareness of the particular needs of Kennesaw's students, faculty, and the community, and many have been held up as exemplars of progressive higher education leadership. For example, in a casebook on excellence in higher education supported by the American Council on Education (ACE), *Searching for Academic Excellence: Twenty Colleges and Universities on the Move and Their Leaders* (1986), Dr. Siegel was commended for her emphasis on teamwork as a means towards institutional planning and for innovative programs such as the Center for Excellence in Teaching and Learning (CETL) and the Center for Personal and Career Counseling (CAPS), which offers students counseling, advising, and placement services. Again, in 1987, the Council for Advancement and Support of Education (CASE) selected Kennesaw as one of three top colleges and universities in a national competition focusing on "The President and the Public." In the fall of 2003 KSU was named by the Policy Center on the First Year of College at Brevard College as one of 12 founding institutions included in its Foundations of Excellence in the First College Year program. *U.S. News and World Report* has also recognized Kennesaw for its first-year experience program. Also in 2003, the RTM Restaurant Group created a $1 million endowment to support a center for the study and promotion of leadership and ethics, now known as the Siegel Institute for Leadership, Ethics, and Character. Dr. Siegel currently holds the Betty L. Siegel Endowed Chair of Leadership, Ethics, and Character, and the institute offers programs and workshops to the university and surrounding community that focus on helping organizations value diversity and promote ethical conduct and leadership in business, non-profit, and governmental organizations.

One of the contributors of this volume, Senator Johnny Isakson, aptly summed up Dr. Siegel's achievements in a statement of recognition on the U.S. Senate floor at the time of her stepping down from the presidency: "She built a [sub]urban university that was nonresidential and commuter into a combination commuter and residential university of renown and respect all over the United States." Though briefly stated, this point represents years of thought, planning, meetings, conversations, negotiations, effort, and energy from Dr. Siegel, all in the service of Kennesaw's students, staff, faculty, and community. In an era when, according to the ACE, the average time in office for college presidents is eight and a half years, her 25 years' tenure is a testament to persistence, intellectual and political acumen, sensitivity, and, without a doubt, a substantial measure of personal charisma.

Over the years, Dr. Siegel's vision and achievements have caught the attention of many community and business groups, and she has received a number of awards for her service to education and to community. Among her awards are the following:

- Distinguished Teacher of the Year at the University of Florida (1969)
- Cobb County Citizen of the Year (1996)
- 1997 Georgia Woman of the Year (Georgia Commission on Women)
- OAK Award (Outstanding Alumni for Kentucky) from the Kentucky Advocates for Higher Education (1998)
- Junior Achievement Business Hall of Fame by the Atlanta Business Chronicle (1999)
- *Atlanta Business Chronicle*'s Cobb County Who's Who and Most Influential Atlantans (multiple years)
- One of *Atlanta Magazine*'s 20 Women Making a Mark on Atlanta
- 100 Most Influential Georgians (named nine times by *Georgia Trend* magazine)
- Women in Business Lifetime Achievement Award
- Peabody Award from the School of Education at the University

of North Carolina—Chapel Hill, the Alumni Association's highest award given to "an outstanding individual who has made an extraordinary impact on the field of education"

- Leita Thompson Achievement Award recognizing Dr. Siegel's support of education for disadvantaged women by the Leitalift Foundation
- Justice Robert Benham Award for "outstanding leadership, service and total commitment to the equality of all citizens" by the Blacks United for Youth of Cobb County, Inc. (2004)
- Northwest Georgia YWCA Lifetime Achievement Award (2005)
- Howard Washington Thurman Ecumenical Award, from Morehouse College's Martin Luther King, Jr. International Chapel, for "contributions to humanity in interfaith, interdenominational and interracial spiritual and ethical development (2005)

This list does little justice to the work that preceded recognition, but, taken as a whole, the awards echo the perennial themes of her life and life's work: service, teamwork and community, leadership as a process of personal and professional development, and stewardship. The contributors to this volume wrote about the same ideas as they drew connections between their careers and private lives and their relationships with the honoree, constructing, if you will, a society of self-aware and conscientious leaders.

A Commitment to Service

In a 2006 interview with *Atlanta-Journal Constititution* reporter Aixa Pascual, Dr. Siegel looked back over her career at Kennesaw and provided an assessment of her administration's achievements. She said, "I'm most proud of what we've done for student success, what we've done in diversity, what we're doing in ethical leadership, what we've done in engagement with the communities we serve." In contrast, she explained that she did *not* want to be remembered "for the buildings . . . [or] just the programs" but for what they "mean to students. We have to have student success as a part of our legacy." This comment shows the president's focus on service as central to her concept of working in academe. Helping the people who come to Kennesaw, whoever they are and wherever they come from, has been an ever-present goal for Dr. Siegel and appears in her advice to new teachers in an article she wrote for *IMPACT* magazine: "To understand teaching as the work of the heart as well as the head is to understand both its relation to our inner lives and its importance as public service" ("Teaching as a Heartfelt Commitment" 1).

Dr. Siegel's colleagues both at Kennesaw and from elsewhere often echoed this theme in their essays. William Purkey, a long-time friend and colleague from her days at the University of Florida, includes a memorable—and funny—anecdote about jointly teaching a class of surly, recalcitrant teachers long ago with Dr. Siegel and trying new strategies for weeks on end to engage the group. Neither ever doubted that they must do everything they could to reach their students, even if the students, who in this case were required to attend, did not want to be reached. Betsy Barefoot, the co-director and senior scholar for the Policy Center on the First Year of College, writes about how she met Dr. Siegel while working on the issue of improving outcomes for beginning college students. Dr. Barefoot commends Dr. Siegel for her eloquent words on this topic and, moreover, for "her actions to transform Kennesaw State University into an institution that holds itself accountable for the success of new students." They share the view "that students matter most in the milieu of higher education and that we should weigh every decision we make in terms of its effect, positive or negative, on students—especially new students who are most at risk."

Nancy King, Vice President for Student Success and Enrollment at KSU, also describes her commitment to service by quoting Dr. Siegel: "Once again I am reminded of the words I've heard Betty Siegel say countless times: 'Service is the rent you pay on the time and space you spend on earth.'" Dr. King's essay traces her own development from a faculty member to an administrator who learns that teaching remains her most important task, even if she is no longer primarily doing it in a traditional classroom. She notes the distinction between a focus on students as learners and students as would-be graduates, positing that teaching students to become learners is certainly as important as ensuring that they earn degrees. She recognizes both the first- and senior-year experience programs as crucial to KSU's mission of service to students and describes its value to her: "What a joy to have a job where I am allowed to see firsthand students discover their capacity to succeed. It is like having a front row seat to watch miracles unfold."

Howard Shealy, Chair of Kennesaw's Department of History and Philosophy, reminisces about the calling to teach that he felt when he joined the faculty at "Harvard in the Pines," a tongue-in-cheek nickname faculty gave to Kennesaw in its early years. Dr. Shealy unpacks the rich meaning of teaching as a "calling," noting that it

> simultaneously suggests the Catholic concept of a vocation, the Calvinist notion that each of us has a role to play in the divine schema that must be carried out with the utmost diligence, and the Renaissance humanist belief that we all have innate talents that should be developed to their fullest if we are to be personally fulfilled and are to contribute fully to society.

His essay provides an account of the early years of Kennesaw College and its culture as well as a narrative of the college's growth. At the end he returns to the value of service as a lesson that faculty must teach and students must learn:

> We have nourished generations of foster sons and daughters intellectually and spiritually and prepared them to lead rich and productive lives. We have taught them that learning does not stop with the attainment of a degree, or even a series of degrees, and we have tried to make them 'good stewards of place' whether that means preserving historic heritage, the natural environment, or human rights.

Dr. Shealy emphasizes that Dr. Siegel has powerfully influenced the culture of KSU in its view of service.

One contributor to the volume personifies the Siegel-KSU focus on service as a lesson to teach and to learn. Betsy Downer Brown is a KSU graduate who worked in Dr. Siegel's office while she was a student. After a brief corporate career, she returned to Kennesaw to become certified to teach high school. Though a devoted and award-winning teacher, she sees clearly the challenges of succeeding as a teacher and, indeed, of succeeding at all. Her essay, a collection of moving anecdotes from "the gritty side of life" she has observed through her role as a teacher, offers glimpses into the sadness, wonder, and charity of a teaching career as she advocates good humor and resiliency.

A similar philosophy emerges in the essay by the renowned former president of both Spelman and Bennett Colleges, Johnnetta Cole. Dr. Cole discusses the principles she depends on for decision making: "the responsibility to empower others"; the requirement of seeing "each individual's humanity, preciousness, and potential for greatness"; and the awareness that "my role is to serve, not to control, or be glorified through the work." Service is the starting point in her essay, and she explains how she has applied it to all the roles and struggles she has faced during her career.

The Inclusion of Others: Teamwork and Community

In her farewell letter to the faculty and staff of Kennesaw, Dr. Siegel attributes all the growth of Kennesaw to "the spirit of creative collaboration that has defined our work at its best." This gracious statement reveals fundamental practices of the culture of Kennesaw under Dr. Siegel's leadership, a team approach to working on goals and an inclusion of the community in campus life and concerns. On occasion, these views have been expressed in a rather folksy idiom, as Joseph Meeks, Dean of the College of the Arts, quotes Dr. Siegel in his essay: "[W]e are altogether better because we are all together." Nonetheless, teamwork and community have been hallmarks of Dr. Siegel's administration, recognized by researchers for ACE. In *Searching for Academic Excellence*, Dr. Siegel discusses her outlook on the benefits of teamwork:

> It seems to me that you need people who can offer different perspectives. People who complement each other, and then you build a team on personal and professional diplomacy. . . . It's popular with some people to be the giant with all the pygmies around them, but the further I get along, the more I realize that a president should know his or her own limitations and get people around them to complement their strengths and weaknesses. (qtd. in Gilley, Fulmer, and Reithingshoefer 109)

At the time of this study in the mid 1980s, the college was recognized for two programs, CETL and the CAPS Center, as "direct results of the team planning concept" (Gilley, Fulmer, and Reithingshoefer 30).

In a lyrical yet scholarly discussion about recognizing the sustaining power of community, Sally Hare, the president of Still Learning, Inc. and the founding director of the Center for Education and Community at Coastal Carolina University, describes the benefits of accepting the importance of community as a guide in all endeavors. Dr. Hare characterizes community as less a "goal to be achieved [than] a gift to be received." Her essay traces how "Community is fundamental to the learning that is the essence of being human. From early childhood, our first work is developing the sense of trust that is essential to being a healthy member of the community."

Although he comes from a very different line of work, Senator Johnny Isakson also stresses community in his essay. After noting how all of his accomplishments stem from "what I learned from others and what others have done for me," he tells a series of interrelated anecdotes about community writ large in citizenship and patriotism. In particular, he is moved by a recognition that our community is made possible by Americans who have served in the armed forces. Isakson concludes by explaining how his awareness of community has motivated him to be an active patriot:

> But just writing a piece is not enough—we have to talk about our patriotism and we have to live it. I'm thankful

I had my moment in time at the grave of Roy Miller, and I hope that sometime in their lives all Americans can have a similar moment in time so that they can gain a perspective, be shocked into reality, and reflect on what a wonderful country this is and on those who gave us a chance to experience it and to love it.

Joel Siegel, a judge and professor as well as Dr. Siegel's husband and soul mate, develops the theory of community in the broadest sense; he sees it as a concept that makes it possible for humans to find meaning in the face of mortality. He explains and advises simultaneously: "It is through the human-derived institutions of government, law, and religion and through the cultural avenues of language, ceremony, ritual, and tradition that we experience the world. We may be marked for oblivion in nature, but human culture makes available to us vast resources (and the only resources) for establishing an identity and for imposing meaning on the stubborn stuff of life." This search for purpose and place, an "ongoing task," leads us to wisdom, or rather, an "understanding [of] who and what we are in relation to our world."

Leadership as Identity and Practice

No doubt because Dr. Siegel has been a leader for so long, she has also long had an intellectual interest in leadership, that abstract term linking notions of identity and behavior together within an individual to enable him or her to move organizations toward goals. In addition to her pivotal work in the establishment of the Institute for Leadership, Character, and Ethics at KSU, in 2003 Dr. Siegel co-authored *Becoming an Invitational Leader: A New Approach to Professional and Personal Success* with Dr. Purkey, which describes their approach to leadership. This book emphasizes how essential it is for a leader to strive for consistency in word and deed, in what one believes and what one does, in how one wants to be and how one is to others: "*Leadership is in large part the product of internal dialogue regarding what we say to ourselves about ourselves, others, and the world*" (39 italics in original). The authors coin the terms "the whispering self" to refer to this ongoing internal dialogue (39-40) and "invitational leadership" to mean the model of behavior that arises from it. In contrast to an authoritative approach, Drs. Purkey and Siegel recommend "invitational leadership [which] involves a generous and genuine turning toward others in empathy and respect, with the ultimate goal of collaborating with them on projects of mutual benefit. The emphasis shifts from command and control to cooperation and communication, from manipulation to cordial summons, from exclusiveness to inclusiveness, from *subordinates* to *associates*" (4).

A number of contributors echoed both the personal and professional dimensions of leadership discussed in Drs. Purkey and Siegel's text. For example, Vice President King, Dean Meeks, Dr. Hare, and Dr. David Siegel, an associate professor in the Department of Educational Leadeship at East Carolina Univeristy, all write passionately about the necessity of finding a balance in one's outlook that helps anyone, but especially a leader, manage the conflicting impulses and demands of one's personal and professional roles. Dr. David Siegel, in his "meditation" on balance calls the task of finding it "an epic struggle to get it right, which entails plenty of experimentation but little in the way of definitive solutions." Similarly, Dr. Hare uses dancing as a metaphor for the act of balancing roles:

> Life is a dance, not a linear uphill battle. It begins as a dance between our role as individual and our role as community member. . . . It's a lifelong dance between who we are and whose we are and what we are here to do, a lifelong dance co-creating our Work in the world, developing our birthright gifts so we can use them in service of the community. Through the process of this lifelong dance, we are constantly constructing and co-constructing the Individual and Community and Work.

Part of the knack of achieving balance, according to Vice President King and Dean Meeks, is knowing one's core values and applying them to all areas of life. Dr. King describes a "balance point" that "allows us to find meaning and common purpose in the many roles we play. Dean Meeks tenderly recalls resonant childhood lessons about planning, improvisation, and collaboration, practices he now recognizes as key to his, and Kennesaw's, achievements.

The personal dimension of leadership often involves spirituality as well. President Cole frankly states that "to attempt to lead without engaging in a quest for personal spiritual development will hardly bring productive results for anyone." She notes the necessity of leaders modeling "the values you wish to support. Indeed, as the saying goes, you can't lead where you won't go."

Seconding this spiritual dimension to leadership, novelist and physician Ferrol Sams borrows the phrase "divine choreography" from a longtime associate to describe how a person who is keenly aware both of oneself and of others can touch lives by using serendipitously the knowledge and skills he or she has acquired:

> Sometimes a series of concrete actions can, in retrospect, appear to be spiritual and have a lasting effect on a person. . . . While it is happening, such an event seems the logical outcome of one's training and an automatic response to circumstance. Looking back, the events appear totally illogical and one's reaction an example of Aristotle's definition of "good."

He draws this lesson from a gripping tale of a medical emergency he happened upon at just the right moment.

Dr. Sams' story connects the character of a leader to the actions that influence and affect others. Dr. Purkey makes a similar point in his essay about the characteristics of cheerful leaders. He reasons,

> cheerful leaders don't take themselves too seriously. They work to savor every moment, to find humor in frustrations, to fight fair, to challenge authority, and to believe that any attempt is a victory. They are reconstructionists, as opposed to participants. They like to make things happen.

After all, leaders must go beyond reflection; they must do. One way leaders practice their craft is to encourage people to belong, sincerely and fully, to an organization, the essence of invitational leadership. Of course, this idea has direct application for college presidents. Dr. Michael Siegel, the director of the Administration of Higher Education Program at Suffolk University, applies the idea to this line of work in his essay. He traces the process by which college presidents "invoke cultural properties such as norms, values, beliefs, artifacts, sagas, and the like to make sense of the environment." He posits that as the "primary culture-bearers" of their institutions, college presidents "must be able to convey respect and an appreciation for the core values and traditions of a college or university" to all stakeholders. This point ties together the two strands of leadership, the strand of identity and the strand of practice. Readers of this volume will see how Dr. Betty Siegel and her family, friends, and colleagues envision both as essential and complexly intertwined.

Stewardship

To what end do leaders strive? Though countless answers to this question are possible, one emerges from the voices in this volume: stewardship. But the definition of stewardship that comes from these pages has multiple dimensions. The first is service to an organization, a theme much in evidence throughout both this volume and Dr. Siegel's career. In addition, stewardship implies two perspectives. One perspective is retrospective and requires the leader's faithfulness to the values and needs of the organization as it currently exists, with a sincere respect for its history and traditions. The other is visionary, having a dream for the growth of the organization as well as a plan with attainable, meaningful goals and pathways for journeying toward these goals. While not applicable only to college presidents, this conception of stewardship is a natural one for all sorts of academic leaders. Dr. Michael Siegel signals these two perspectives of stewardship in his essay title, "Nostalgia and Renewal: The Role of the College President in Shaping Campus Culture," and the body of his article builds a compelling case for their significance. Without both, he suggests, a president is unlikely to steer well or long. Dr. Barefoot, Vice President King, and Dr. David Siegel also investigate the issue of how best to nurture the various members of a university community, recognizing how essential it is for a teacher to understand where students "are" to identify how to help them achieve their goals.

In looking back over her years as Kennesaw's president, Dr. Siegel has chosen the noun "steward" to characterize her role: "I've tried to be a steward of the place. I like that term," she said during an interview (Pascual). And it's clear that she has worked with a dual perspective: "What I have so loved and hope I've been effective in," [Dr. Siegel] says, "is being able to see what has been the past as well as to see into the future. And to help us use what we have learned in learning more" (Edwards 11).

This volume explores the life lessons that Dr. Siegel and her colleagues have learned. It also presents these lessons for readers' own reflection in memorable, often amusing, and sometimes deeply moving essays. As each of us struggles to achieve a balanced perspective on the trials and challenges of our personal and professional lives, we can surely learn from those, like Dr. Betty Siegel, who have wintered into wisdom.

References

American Council on Education. "College Presidents Aging and Holding Jobs Longer According to a New Report on the College Presidency from the American Council on Education." (press release) 12 February 2007. 18 June 2007 <www.acenet.edu/AM/Template.cfm?Section=Press_Releases2&Template=/CM/ContentDisplay.cfm&CONTENTID=20430>.

Beowulf: A Verse Translation. Trans. Seamus Heaney. Ed. Daniel Donoghue. Norton Critical Edition. New York: Norton, 2002.

Edwards, Dianna. "Once Upon a Pasture," *Summit Magazine,* Fall 2001, 9-11.

Gilley, J. Wade, Kenneth A. Fulmer, and Sally J. Reithlingshoefer. *Searching for Academic Excellence: Twenty Colleges and Universities on the Move and their Leaders.* New York: American Council on Education and Macmillan, 1986.

Isakson, Johnny. "U.S. Senator Johnny Isakson (R-GA) Floor Statement Congratulating Dr. Betty Siegel: Remarks as Delivered on the Senate Floor." 26 May 2005. 6 June 2007. <isakson.senate.gov/floor/2005/052605siegel.htm>

Pascual, Aixa M. "Betty Siegel: KSU's Woman of Vision," *Atlanta Journal-Constitution,* 2 February 2006: 1JF. LexisNexis, 7 June 2007.

Purkey, William W. and Betty L. Siegel. *Becoming an Invitational Leader: A New Approach to Professional and Personal Success.* Atlanta: Humanics Trade Group, 2003.

Siegel, Betty L. "Teaching as a Heartfelt Commitment: A Message to New Teachers," IMPACT, n.d.

---. Letter to Kennesaw State University Colleagues, Kennesaw State University, Kennesaw, GA. 30 June 2006.

"As you have done it unto the least of these . . .": A Guiding Ethic for Freshman Educators

Betsy O. Barefoot

When I entered the career in higher education that has occupied the last 20 years of my life, I did so without really thinking about whether or how this career would connect to my spiritual self or my basic values. Like many other job seekers, I found an opening that seemed interesting and relevant to my education, and the rest is history. I've been lucky. My recent life as an advocate for the importance of the first college year has afforded me numerous opportunities to tap into my own sense of ultimate purpose and into my beliefs. And never has pursuing this career required that I abandon or ignore my most deeply held values or that I become less than authentically me.

My work has given me many opportunities to reach out to others and to proclaim "justice for freshmen"—higher education's underdogs. My work has also brought me in contact with many educators around the world who share my values, and together we have formed a strong community that is bound through a collective positive regard for entering students of all types, levels of ability, and prior experience. It is through this work that I met President Betty Siegel who shares my passion and commitment to the beginning college student. President Siegel has written and spoken eloquently about the importance of the first year. But her actions to transform Kennesaw State University into an institution that holds itself accountable for the success of new students have spoken even more loudly than her words.

For all who enter colleges and universities, the first year is one of life's most significant transitions. And transitions are difficult—whether they involve redefining home and family, separating from loved ones, moving to another location, or entering a new cultural environment where the rules are different and threatening. Many in my generation remember the transition to college as harsh and unforgiving—you sink or you swim.

Historically, college freshmen have had the "least" of what the academy values—the least knowledge, the least experience, and the least self-confidence. And these students have often received the least attention from their host institutions. It has been all too common for them to be herded into enormous class sections, forced to live in the most undesirable campus accommodations, and taught by hastily hired part-time faculty or graduate students as a money-saving strategy for the institution.

But through the years, educators who work closely with freshmen have learned that if we are to achieve our societal goal of broader educational access for "all God's children," we must focus on the quality of the beginning experience and do a better job of providing safety nets when new students stumble as well as clear pathways to a more meaningful life. And for some of us, service to "the least of these" has become not merely a rewarding life's work, but a calling that we pursue with missionary zeal.

Maintaining a singular focus on freshmen, however, is a calling that comes with numerous challenges. Those of us in American higher education who advocate for the importance of the first year frequently find ourselves in conflicts with others about what matters most for our campuses and how precious institutional resources should be spent. Occasionally, we are vilified in the press or in academic journals for what are perceived as our attempts to "lower standards" and "destroy traditions" by offering new students a high level of academic and social support. But in spite of opposition we continue our work, both individually and collectively, believing the greatest good comes in service to students.

As I ponder how and why this focus on the first year has been successful in uniting and empowering a worldwide community of educators, I believe it is because we are bonded through a common ethic that influences our day-to-day interactions with students, with each other, and with the world at large. This ethic, represented by the title of this essay, holds that students matter most in the milieu of higher education and that we should weigh every decision we make in terms of its effect, positive or negative, on students—especially new students who are most at risk. This ethic rests on adherence to certain ideals. While none of us can claim practicing these ideals in every single circumstance, I believe they are critically important to the ultimate impact of our work.

Respect for Students

In my work in American higher education, I can recall visiting many colleges and universities that were characterized by a genuine respect for students. Conversely I can recall a few college campuses where respect for students was in short supply and where "student bashing" was the rule of the day. A special campus where faculty and staff have the highest levels of respect for students is LaGuardia Community College in the Borough of Queens, New York. LaGuardia is a microcosm of the world; the student population is comprised of students from 170 countries. Many of those students are facing incredible barriers—little prior education, family and work responsibilities, and poor English language skills. But LaGuardia faculty are quick to describe their students as "heroic." Many who teach at LaGuardia receive job offers from more prestigious institutions, but they stay because they are making a difference, because they are witnessing the power of education to transform lives. Not every LaGuardia student is successful academically, but every student benefits by an atmosphere characterized by genuine respect.

Cooperation with Other Members of the Community

Higher education can be rightfully characterized as a competitive world where institutions, faculty, and students compete with each other for status and power. The community of freshman educators is just the opposite. Cooperation with each other is the norm. Through listservs, large conferences, and other forms of communication, community members are willing to offer advice, assistance, personal experience, and when necessary, a shoulder to cry on. For the past several years, annual conferences on the first-year experience— attended by higher education faculty, staff, and administrators from all over the world—have featured a special session on "spirituality, authenticity, and wholeness in higher education" (National Resource Center 74). These sessions, in which Betty Siegel was a frequent participant, have provided a safe place for conference attendees to talk with others about not only routine issues and challenges, but also their most deeply held values and how those values intersect with their work lives. Participants have felt free to share their authentic selves, their concerns about the purpose and value of their work, and how their job enables or challenges their exploration of spirituality. And they have listened and responded to others with caring and respect.

Honesty (with Compassion)

No one would disagree that honesty should guide the work of freshman educators. However, the goal of honesty is not as straightforward as it might seem. While it is easy to assert the importance of being honest about one's own accomplishments or knowledge, it is occasionally difficult to determine how honest one should be when advising or counseling new students. Many freshman educators have, on occasion, found themselves in the uncomfortable position of either bolstering or dashing students' false hopes and dreams. Neither position feels right. What kinds of feedback do students need and deserve? While there is no simple answer to this question, in general they need competent counsel that is delivered with support and caring. We can help students explore their strengths, acknowledge their limitations, and aim for the stars (but always with Plan B in their back pockets).

Authenticity

Because of the competitive pressures of higher education, faculty and administrators are occasionally guilty of pretense—claiming knowledge they don't have in order to gain "respect," claiming success without evidence to support their claims, and pretending self-assurance they don't feel. While these behaviors are certainly not limited to the ivory tower, they are somehow especially troubling in college and university settings where "truth" is the ostensible goal. In order to help students accept themselves and acknowledge their strengths and weaknesses, it is important that we represent ourselves as authentic human beings who are neither perfect nor all-knowing. Students will gravitate to those among us who are most authentic. As we are comfortable in our own skin, so students will learn to accept themselves as they are while believing in their potential for positive change.

Empathy

New students often feel "marginal" in the world of higher education. Many can't imagine that their professors ever failed a course or engaged in behavior they later regretted. Some new students have a deep belief that their college admission was a giant mistake— that they will be discovered for the frauds they surely are. Important to working effectively with new students is the ability to empathize with their perceptions of themselves and the world. Sometimes this requires a "trip back in time"—conjuring up those thoughts, feelings, and events that were part of one's own transition experiences. Stephen Brookfield, speaker and writer in the areas of teaching and adult education, suggests building empathy for the student experience by reentering the classroom as a learner, not a teacher. Each year, Brookfield, selects a new experience in learning—something out of his comfort zone—and he becomes, once again, the "marginal" student with all the feelings of inferiority and marginality. Brookfield maintains that these experiences give him a level of empathy for the new student experience that he can gain in no other way.

Assertiveness

While few of us enjoy conflict, there are those times when we must stand our ground in support of our values. My colleague and spouse, John Gardner, frequently argues that institutions do what they value. He would add that colleges and universities generally find the resources to do what they value most. For the community of freshman educators, values conflicts, so rife in American education, often become the most frustrating part of our work. Many of us have found ourselves in the middle of successful initiatives on behalf of new students only to have our positions and programs eliminated or drastically downsized because of a shift in institutional values.

The prestige that accrues with research dollars, massive athletic facilities, voluminous libraries, and restrictive admissions policies is the siren song for many institutions—even those that were established to serve as the point of entry for students who were historically underrepresented in higher education. As colleges and universities focus on the outward symbols of institutional worth, the inward symbols—student learning and progress—fall by the wayside.

In community, we as freshman educators are able to share struggles and frustrations, assist each other in finding objective evidence to support the value of the work we do, work together to negotiate the never-ending campus political battles, and remind each other of the ultimate value of our work to our students and the larger society. And then it falls to us to be assertive advocates for students on our own campuses in the face of competing institutional priorities.

Resisting the Abuse of Power

In her provocative book, *A Life in School: What the Teacher Learned,* well-known professor and literary critic Jane Tompkins, talks about the lure of power inherent in the teaching relationship. She recalls her earliest memories of school and how she wished to identify with the teacher, to subordinate her own thoughts and feelings to those of the teacher, because the teacher had power. She goes on to describe her fiercely competitive experience in graduate school when power was abused frequently and yet was the brass ring that all students prized.

Teachers at any level have enormous power and influence over students' lives. For better or worse, many of us are put on pedestals by our students—they believe what we say, they pattern their behavior after ours, and they yearn for our approval. Such power is both advantageous and dangerous. We can influence students to trust themselves and honor their intellectual voice—or through our arrogance, we can convince them that the only voice that matters is ours.

Mary Belenky, Blythe Clinchy, Nancy Goldberger, and Jill Tarule, in their seminal book, *Women's Ways of Knowing: The Development of Self, Voice, and Mind*, write specifically about the learning process for women of all ages and life stages. In their research they found that many women feel dwarfed by authority and "voiceless" in its presence. Only in a cooperative learning environment that levels power dynamics are many women able to find and trust their own intellectual capabilities.

Those of us who work with first-year students find these characteristics applicable not only to women, but to men as well, and we strive to empower all our students to trust themselves and their views of the world. The lines between teacher and learner become blurred as everyone in the learning setting becomes both the giver and the receiver of knowledge.

The appropriate use of power also requires that we occasionally "sit on our wisdom." It is not easy to watch students experience the same struggles we endured. So often it would be so easy to give them the unequivocal answer to a question or to resolve a dilemma on their behalf, but when we are committed to student learning, we acknowledge that the most significant learning comes through life experience—making mistakes, experiencing disappointment, and surviving failure.

A Focus on the Whole Person—
Ourselves and Our Students

Parker Palmer, internationally known educational writer and scholar, reminds us that our work with students involves more than transmitting objective information. He observes that if our teaching deals more in external facts than in inner wisdom, we are "the most dangerous creatures on earth: people who know much about the outer world but who know little about their inner selves, who have technical competence but no understanding of their own drives and desires." Much about our current culture does not value a focus on the inner self. Personal worth tends to be measured in terms of outward appearance, possessions, and in the case of college and university educators, scholarly credentials and productivity. For many of us in higher education, it is far easier to focus our "microscopes" on objective phenomena, the world around us, than it is to turn the focus inward. But those who are able to work most successfully with new students are those with a deep understanding of themselves, their inner thoughts, feelings, motivations, and their own sense of spirituality.

Working successfully with new students also means knowing about them as whole individuals—their family history and heritage, prior lives, current activities, and their dreams for the future. Learning about students' personal lives beyond the classroom is not always easy. Often students are hesitant to share what may seem to them an unimportant life. Some college faculty and administrators also find that developing relationships with students is difficult and uncomfortable. But research on teaching styles finds that many students learn best in a "relational" atmosphere—a setting in which students and teachers know something about each other's personal lives and experience. Establishing appropriate connections with students as whole individuals is an important part of the work we do.

As part of a whole-person approach to students is the importance of allowing them a safe place to explore issues of spirituality. In national surveys of entering first-year college students completed over the past several years, students themselves have expressed their own desire for exploration of spirituality, which they differentiate from "being religious." In the 2006 book, *Encouraging Authenticity and Spirituality in Higher Education*, Arthur Chickering, Jon Dalton, and Liesa Stamm state, "spirituality is commonly described by college students as transformation, authenticity, life force, transcendence, and peak experience. Such terms . . . convey the notion that spiritual experience can be anything that expresses deep meaning. Spirituality can be a slippery terrain unless its meaning is clearly defined and distinguished from religion" (162).

Some students find freedom to explore these areas in a religious community, but for others, these gatherings—whether in traditional churches or religiously affiliated student groups—become too restrictive and narrow. Whatever our personal belief system, it is important that we offer students a non-judgmental place to explore their own thoughts and feelings about spirituality. As Chickering and his colleagues argue, "When we tolerate a bifurcated life in the academy that honors the life of the mind but relegates the realm of spirituality to the purely private domain, we make higher education less welcoming and engaging for students" (164). The damage is that students are encouraged to "lead duplicitous lives" when reason is prized above emotion and detachment above connection to others (164).

Concluding Thoughts

The title of this festschrift, *Wintering into Wisdom*, acknowledges the hope and the belief that as we age and gain life experience, we become more wise. Those of us who are approaching the winter of our lives find solace in the work of Erik Erickson who argued that if we are lucky, as we age we can look back on our lives with happiness and feel fulfilled with a deep sense that our lives have had meaning and we've made a contribution to the lives of others.

Accepting, owning, and then sharing the wisdom that comes with age is one of life's greatest joys and most significant responsibilities. We who have been entrusted with the education of the next generation of the world's citizens are responsible for imparting not only knowledge, but also the values through which our planet can continue to thrive. We must share our wisdom as we pass the baton to those who will come after us. The challenges will be no less, but the continuing opportunity to minister to new college students—"the least of these"—is an opportunity to transform the face of American higher education, our nation, and our world.

Works Cited

Belenky, Mary, Blythe Clinchy, Nancy Goldberger, and Jill Tarule. *Women's Way of Knowing: The Development of Self, Voice, and Mind.* 1986. New York: Basic-Perseus, 1997.

Chickering, Arthur W., John C. Dalton, and Liesa Stamm. *Encouraging Authenticity and Spirituality in Higher Education.* San Francisco: Jossey-Bass, 2006.

National Resource Center for the First-Year Experience and Students in Transition. *Program: 25th Annual Conference on the First-Year Experience.* Columbia, SC: U of SC, 2006.

Palmer, Parker. "Teaching in the Face of Fear." *The National Teaching & Learning Forum* 6.5 (1997). The National Teaching & Learning Forum. 1997. 24 July 2006 <http://www.ntlf.com/html/pi/9708/palmer2.htm>.

Tompkins, Jane. *A Life in School: What the Teacher Learned.* 1996. New York: Perseus, 2006.

Risks and Rewards

Betsy Downer Brown

Since I don't believe in reincarnation, I know that I will walk this earth only once. That's a scary thought, and I don't want to miss a single thing during my visit. I have an adventurous spirit trapped inside a cowardly body, and I enjoy watching others live more exciting and daring lives than my own. I walk to the precipice with them, but when they jump, I'm not even at the edge yet. I might look over the side—if there's a sturdy handrail. My brain is full of creative thoughts that I gladly give away to others who are more willing to run with them. I get complete fulfillment (and safety) from this arrangement, and I don't plan to change. It's my grand experiment! If I can get vicarious experience from watching everyone else take risks, I can live safely to one hundred. So what if all my friends will be dead! I'll have lots of stories for my grandchildren.

The words "thrill-seeking behavior" do not register in my internal vocabulary; I most certainly do not bungee jump into anything that has not been thoroughly tested by the AMA or the USDA or OSHA. I drove a boxy Volvo station wagon for years before I was married and became a mother, and I won't eat oysters no matter what letters are in or are not in the name of the month. I won't even ride in a convertible, and I'm becoming more and more leery of the concept of flying. Though I am certain that I am in need of a pedicure more than any woman I know, I won't soak my feet in a plastic tub used by countless others. My friends get so exasperated with me: "They clean those tubs between clients, Betsy." And I say, "Have you actually seen them scrubbing with Clorox? No. I didn't think so."

I wouldn't call myself neurotic, though I do have quite a fondness for Purell hand sanitizer. I think I've just seen and heard so many truly sad stories that I try to protect myself and my precious cub from anything harmful that I can see coming. It's the sneak attack that will get me someday, I'm sure.

This all sounds well and good, but (Surprise!) I'm not able to protect myself as fully as I had planned. While I can stay away from the physical dangers involved in riding a Harley or diving with sharks, I can't shield myself from emotional pain. And I've found that I don't want to.

I never had much exposure to horror or true sadness until I started my career in education. And before I go any further, let me assure you that I love my job! Just because I have been introduced to reality does not mean I regret it. Most of my life experiences have been wholesome and happy, and I'm forever grateful for that leg up I've had on the rest of the world. When I see something that shocks or hurts me, the expressions I wear on my face are the tell-tale signs of my outrage at the world. I cannot hide my feelings, and I often feel real physical pain when I hear stories of others whose lives have been harder than mine. I used to put my big toe into their oceans of sadness, and then I retreated to the safe, clean world I had always known. Now I climb into the water with others, but I never take my eye off the shore.

Defining Me

I euphemistically refer to my peculiar choices and opinions as quirks of personality, and I remember the day, years ago, when Dr. Betty Siegel wrinkled up her nose into a smile, tapped me on the forehead, and called me "quirky." I wore that compliment like my own Miss America crown. I still wear it proudly, and I love explaining to others how and why it fits so well. I received this compliment when I was very young, and my profession has helped this part of my nature to grow. I take in so much information that my head spins with some of it. After witnessing something particularly disturbing, I rebound with a quick and frozen smile on my face while my brain tries to find a way to assimilate the images and feelings.

The moment Dr. Siegel made this observation about my nature we were talking about something important (that I have now forgotten), and I offered to share my bag of gummy bears as I was listening to her. It must have struck her as funny that I was having an adult conversation while wolfing down children's candy, but she quickly came to understand the sweet joy these bears can bring to daily life.

I worked in Dr. Siegel's office when I was a student at Kennesaw, and though I knew I was fortunate to work closely with such a successful and visionary person, I couldn't have known then what a wonderful example she would be for me in my personal life. I would never have guessed that I would turn out to be a busy working mother, and I didn't know that I would wait until my thirties to have my first child—just like Dr. Siegel. I also didn't know that I would devote my life to education. On days when I can't handle one more helping on my loaded-down plate, I think of how Dr. Siegel has always been much busier than I am. (And look how her kids turned out!) She gives me inspiration on a daily basis. I hope she's proud of me, even though I haven't made time to work on my doctorate yet.

I remember buying a couple of fresh bags of my favorite gummy bears one day as I was preparing to go on a trip with Dr. Siegel. She was scheduled to deliver a speech in Augusta, Georgia, and I knew we would have a long and late drive down Interstate 20. I was 20 or 21, but my parents were worried about two women driving on the highway late at night. They made me take a pistol with us in the car, and I'll never forget the look on Dr. Siegel's face when she saw that gun. Neither of us knew what to do with it—it wasn't even loaded—but it made my parents feel that we could adequately scare someone with it. So we packed unloaded heat, ate German gummy bears, and barreled down the road telling stories. She was so right; "quirky" is the perfect word.

Career and Family

When I was a child, my parents shielded me from the unpleasantness of life, but my career has given me a front-row view of those not so fortunate. My mom encouraged me to be more like Shirley Feeney than Laverne DiFazio and to marry Richie Cunningham as opposed to The Fonz, and I'm proud, as an adult, to live an almost regret-free life. While I was encouraged to watch *Little House on the Prairie* and forbidden to watch *Three's Company*, many of my students' lives look just like a *Jerry Springer* show or, at best, a tear-streaked episode of *Dr. Phil*.

Precisely because my mother and both of my grandmothers were teachers, I decided to work in the business world. When I graduated from Kennesaw State College in 1989, I worked for three months in corporate America. Like Pip in *Great Expectations*, I quit because "my way of life lay stretched out straight before me" (Dickens 107), and the lifelong confinement of a career scared me to death. In short, my cubicle was too small, my headset was too tight, the sound of the fax machine was too loud, and my lunch hour was too expensive.

My father told me he would pay for me to go back to college if and only if I would become a teacher. When I asked why, he said teaching would "provide a nice second income" for my family in case of emergency. He is, by the way, a true gentleman of the South and was not speaking to me in a condescending voice. He was simply recommending what had worked so well in his marriage and his parents' marriage. I jumped at the offer to crawl back into the comfortable bed of academic life and pull the covers over my head for two more years.

After finishing college (again) and finding my first teaching job, I awakened with a start. Talk about confinement in a career! What was I thinking when I agreed to become a public school teacher? I—literally—haven't visited the restroom at will for 14 years! And that "nice little second income" thing didn't seem one bit funny when my husband made less money than I did for the first three years of our marriage. But slowly, calmly, finally, I realized my father had guided me into the coolest fire he could find. He knew that I was drawn to comedy, downright absurdity, and the unlovable souls who sadly drift among us, and I am, at my core, a teacher.

I used to be a really good teacher before I became a wife and a mother. Sometimes it's not clear when one role starts and another begins. I cannot count the times I have held my car's remote door-locker up to my classroom door and tried to click my way inside. (Probably the same number of times I've tried to use my classroom key to unlock the door to my house.) Some part of my subconscious is obviously confused about where I am and where I'm going most of the time. I mother my students and teach my son, and I try to find time for my wonderful, workaholic husband who struggles even harder to find time for me.

I felt guilty about this blending of roles until recently. The thought that I had chosen to nurture other people's children for more hours each day than I spend with my own child seriously wounded my motherly self-esteem. But now that my son has started school, I'm just plain grateful that his teacher/mother has made that same choice in her own life. Surely it'll all come out in the wash.

I need to teach my son all that I've learned, and I want to teach my students more than the state-required basics. The best lessons I have to share have come from my relationships with other people and the places where my life touches theirs. Jane Austen labeled life as "a quick succession of busy nothings," but I have to disagree (104). Even though I'm as caught up as anyone else in the trivialities that make life so busy, I am struck daily by the symbiotic relationship I have with others. If I didn't have the joy and pain of being involved in the lives of others, I really would be in sad shape. I get up and go to work and go happily home again simply because I love the people in both places. Humanity is the only risk I take.

Specifics

I have a shoebox of pictures, notes, and letters from former students that I cherish more than just about anything I own. Through their words, I am confident that I have enriched their lives as they have enriched mine. I have a beautiful "Teacher of the Century" plaque on my classroom wall that was presented to me by some loving and supportive students, and it means more to me than any actual award ever could. And the well-planned classroom birthday parties I have been truly surprised by over the years have given me the confidence to know that I am important to my students. These numerous positive experiences give me assurance that I have chosen the right place to spend my energies. The real-life lessons, though, come from the gritty side of life. I think of the wonderful memories and smile to myself, but the harder memories are like scabs that I try not to pick at too often.

A few experiences have been large enough to provide leftovers. This doggie bag I bring home from life each day has nourished a thousand interesting phone conversations with friends, a million pleading prayers to the Almighty, and countless lectures in the classroom. My students always listen best when I chuck the lesson plan and tell a personal story. Whether the stories are about other students or about my real life, I think these life lessons are the best of what I serve on my platter of experience. Just as tragedies always outsell comedies at the box office, these sad stories are always favorites with my students. I change people's names when I tell their stories to truly protect them—and to selfishly keep the original version perfect and untouched just for me.

Jeremy

Jeremy was a 19-year-old freshman. He had been unable to complete ninth-grade English five previous times, and I was determined to help him pass my class. He had severe problems with personal hygiene; therefore, he had no friends, and I don't think the teachers tried too hard to go the extra mile for him. It was the 90's, and he really liked 80's music—further making him an outcast to his peers but permanently cementing his relationship with me. We traded cassette tapes back and forth, and I tried to reach out to him however I could.

I found the nerve to speak to him about bathing, and then I asked him why he did so poorly in school. He told me he was possessed by a demon who flew in an open bedroom window years before. We discussed this phenomenon at length, and one Monday morning he told me he had been to Alabama for an exorcism the weekend before. I am very proud to report that I did not laugh.

Unfortunately, I didn't see much of a change in Jeremy after the demon was expelled. When I called his father to discuss his poor progress, his father was obviously drunk. He asked me if I would like to go, I believe the term was, *honky-tonkin'* with him. He started to explain, "Me and his momma is havin' troubles . . . ." I didn't mention this to Jeremy who soon quit school. The last time I saw him, he was stocking shelves at Kroger—and his body odor was nonexistent: success on a small scale.

Suzie

Suzie came to me in ninth grade as well. To date, she is the second-smartest student I have ever taught. Her overall sadness piqued my curiosity from day one, but I tried not to ask personal questions. She alluded to problems at home in her writing, so I referred her to the counselor's office. She told them nothing, but I knew she was lying. The counselors made a referral to the Department of Family and Children Services (DFACS), and the case was investigated and dropped.

Six long years later, I got a call from the district attorney's office asking questions about Suzie. After all this time, she had finally reported her father's abuse. I was being called to testify about what I suspected so many years before. Her father, a physician, had repeatedly raped her, sedated and held her captive in his basement, impregnated her, and performed a subsequent abortion. This last event had finally given Suzie the strength to call 911. I followed my instincts, but it took years to know I had been right.

When I tell this story to young people, I edit out the most disturbing parts. Suzie moved to California after her father went to prison, and I have lost touch with her. She wanted to leave all of the old memories behind, and I hope she never looks back.

Antonio

The district attorney's office called again a few years later; I was being called to testify against one of my own students. I had overheard Antonio casually (and callously, it turns out) mention his desire to kill a female student in the class. I made the required report to the office even though I thought he was just blowing off steam, but I was completely wrong. He had participated in the gang-rape of a female student the weekend before, and he had cut two fingers off of another student at the same event. When the gang found out that I would be testifying, they posted a member outside of my home. I was advised by the sheriff's department to move in with my parents, and they gave me a deputy escort until the trial was over. Antonio was sentenced to time in youth detention, and he never finished high school.

Why was my first impulse to think Antonio was innocent that day in the classroom? I didn't even know our school had any gang members! It took me more than one time to learn this lesson about blind trust: the words "young" and "innocent" do not always go together.

Kevin

Kevin was an open and friendly senior with a bad case of "senioritis." He was good-natured and easy to teach. One day he told me that he wrote me a poem. He looked very proud of himself as he watched me read it:

A Little Blonde Teacher

I like the way the
little blonde teacher teaches.
I like the way she
gets mad. I like the way
my little blonde teacher

floats around the room.
She's so cute; she's so nice.
But what I like best
is to see her face
in a meat grinder, or
her whole body flying out
of a windshield all mangled and
broken up. Hope she never wakes
up.

From that moment, I have not believed that the eyes are the windows to the soul because Kevin looked perfectly sane as I stared at him in horror. He told the counselor he was just kidding, and he was back in my class the next day. I keep a copy of this poem taped to my board to help remind me of what may be out there in front of me.

Katarina

Katarina, a ninth grader, was absent once or twice a week, and she often came to school with bruises. When I asked about them, she would roll her eyes and say, "Damn coffee table." Back to the counselor I went, and DFACS finally made a home visit. They reported that everything seemed fine. When they made a follow-up visit a few weeks later, Katarina's mom, a single mother, decided that she was being harassed by the system. She withdrew Katarina from school and decided to teach her at home.

Then the mother called me to ask a favor. She wanted me to bring Katarina some books and materials and sit down and talk to her about scope and sequence for the remainder of the course. I asked and received permission from my principal to make the visit, and I asked my mom and sister to come along for moral support. I assumed the mother was the abuser, and I was scared to face her alone. When we arrived at the house, I learned that the coffee table was definitely not the reason for Katarina's bruises. The home—in a $300,000-$400,000 neighborhood—did not contain one single piece of furniture. The carpet looked and smelled as if it had been trampled by a pack of wet dogs, and that, along with the walls, was all there was.

Katarina stood in a corner, and her mother did not make excuses for the condition of the house. She invited me to stand at the kitchen counter with her and look at the materials. When my mom, sister, and I left the house, we didn't talk about what we saw. I still don't know what they think.

I never saw Katarina again, but she called me once during my planning period a few years later. She was silly and giggly on the phone and admitted to being dead drunk at ten o'clock in the morning. I asked her to call back when she was sober, but she never did. I would hate to know what was really happening at Katarina's house.

Sam

I'm old-fashioned enough to still put my students in alphabetical order from Day One, and Sam sat in the middle of the middle row. (For those of you who find me too rigid, I do move the desks around for cooperative grouping.) Sam was quiet and shy, and he never looked me in the eye. He was a handsome young man from Pakistan, and I only got to know him through his writing. He never talked in class, and when I called home, I found that his mother did not speak English. I reported him to the counselor and was told that Sam did, indeed, speak English.

He didn't turn in many assignments, but he was always writing in class. When I walked the aisles, I saw his violent depictions of people being tortured. He drew burning American flags and screaming children and machine guns. What I had taken as shyness turned out to be silent aggression: Sam hated Americans, and he had little or no respect for women. He refused to talk about his beliefs, and he was the coldest person I have ever known. I sent him back to the counselor both for his failing grades—his average in my class was a

7—and for his frightening beliefs. We had a conference to discuss his grades, and his mom came and tried her best to participate. In a rare moment of cooperation, Sam told us that his father was in Hamburg on business. When I asked what type of work his father did, Sam told us that he didn't know.

Sam failed my class, and I never saw him again after the final exam in May 2001. After 9/11, I thought of him immediately. His kind of hatred and violence is not self-taught, and I wondered again what his father was doing in Germany. The day I heard about a terror cell that had been located in Hamburg, I went to another teacher who had taught (and worried about) Sam. She volunteered to call the FBI, and I'm glad she did.

Judy

I was lecturing one day, and I noticed that one of my students had a bottle of nail polish remover sitting on her desktop. She wasn't using it, thank goodness, so I didn't say anything about it. I just went on with the lesson. All of a sudden, I saw her pick up the bottle, open the lid, and drink the entire contents in a large gulp. I ran across the room and grabbed the empty bottle from her hands; I smelled it because I was just sure she had filled it with water or something innocuous. I was wrong. Again. Judy had indeed swallowed an entire bottle of nail polish remover. I wrapped my hand around her tiny wrist and ran all the way to the office with her behind me. Someone called 911, and she was taken away in an ambulance.

She came back to class a few days later, and we had a long talk. Her excuse for taking the toxic drink was that she was depressed because her parents had found out she was using drugs. They were planning to send her to Ridgeview, a local substance-abuse rehabilitation center, and she didn't want to leave her friends. Her parents won the struggle, and she withdrew from school that week.

The next fall, Judy appeared in my class again. She had not earned any credits the year before, so she was a freshman again. Her parents told me that she was still struggling with her addictions, but the doctors believed she was ready to come back to school. It soon became obvious that Judy was pregnant. I was so scared for her baby, but she had a healthy pregnancy from the looks of things. Judy could not have weighed 90 pounds before the baby, and the pregnancy actually made her look healthy. Her skin cleared and her attitude brightened.

The baby came at the end of the school year, and Judy brought her to school during teacher post-planning week. I saw a beautiful little baby girl with some serious physical deformities, and Judy said that she didn't understand why her baby had been born with these problems; she guessed it was just bad luck.

Henry

I once visited a murderer in jail, and he was one of the nicest people I have ever known. Henry was my grandfather's best friend for 50 years or so, and he lived in a little house just off of the edge of my grandfather's property in Mississippi. Papa and Henry favored the Braves and the Cubs over any other ball clubs, and Henry helped Papa with his yard and his ancient Oldsmobile. One Saturday night, Henry was drinking in his little house, and another weekend reveler came knocking at his door. The friend pulled out a gun for some reason, and Henry, with his own ready pistol, shot him dead.

I happened to be visiting my grandfather during this time, and I went to the jail with my aunt to take Henry a plate of food. The jailer let us go right back to the cell and deliver Henry's supper. We had a good time talking, and I remember feeling torn inside because I loved a murderer. Henry pled not guilty by reason of insanity, and he spent a year in a mental hospital.

Now, years later, I pass the jail in my town twice a day. (It's on a major thoroughfare, placed by civic leaders hoping to discourage people from participating in activities that would send them there.) The windows in the cells are long and narrow, and I think about the people inside who have such a tiny view of the outside world.

My son points, "There's the big house, Mommy." Oddly enough, he named it that because of its sheer size and before ever hearing the slang terminology. When he asks why people go to jail, I tell him it is because they make bad decisions. I believe this is true for 90 percent of the people inside, and I don't want him to know about the other 10 percent yet. He'll find out for himself.

John

One night I was on the way home from a master's class at Southern Polytechnic State University. I was teaching full time and taking classes in the evenings and on Saturdays, and this particular night I left class at 10 p.m. It was cold and rainy, and I was ready to get home as fast as possible. As I approached a red light about halfway home, I noticed a police car had pulled someone over in the middle lane. I was directly next to the two cars, waiting for the light to turn green. The policeman got out of his car and advanced to the window of the car in front of him. I watched the door fly open and the passenger start beating the policeman with his own night stick. The policeman fell to the ground just as my light turned green.

I pulled over into an empty parking lot and called 911. I hung up as soon as I heard sirens approaching, and I saw more action on the road. Two men who were walking home from work on this cold night intervened on behalf of the policeman and were able to put the attacker in the back of the police car. By the time more policemen and an ambulance arrived, it was obvious that the policeman was badly beaten.

I went to visit him at the hospital the next day, and I found out at that time that I knew him! We went to high school together, and I had not recognized him in the dark. This experience still bothers me because watching the dark side triumph over the light is not easy to witness in real life. But the heroes of the night were later honored by the city, and that restored my faith a little.

Final Comments

Some people stop living when life disappoints them, and I have seen this happen in teenagers, senior citizens, and everyone in between. It's not that I haven't had my moments of doubt and self-pity, but I just don't want to waste more time on the bad things; they have taken up enough of my almost-40 years.

I've had a gun pointed at me by a drug dealer, I've lost three-fourths of the blood in my body from a golf cart accident, I (and my son) survived a hemorrhage during pregnancy, and I've had my heart broken twice. As much as I do not want to repeat any of these experiences, they have enhanced my ability to handle the responsibilities of my life. If I can still make sense of life after touching sadness (and I've left out the worst stories that I'm not able to discuss for both legal reasons and personal promises), then I know how resilient I have become. I have gained courage, perseverance, and confidence by basically just doing my job.

I won't say that I'm ready to hunt tiger or wild boar, and I'm not going to stop using hand sanitizer by the gallon. But the next time I drive the Pacific Coast Highway, I'm going to do it in a Mini Cooper convertible. My mother will warn me not to throw caution to the wind, but I'll promise her that I won't get any crazier than that.

Works Cited

Austen, Jane. *Mansfield Park.* 1814. *The Oxford Illustrated Jane Austen.* Ed. R.W. Chapman. Oxford: Oxford UP, 1966.

Dickens, Charles. *Great Expectations.* 1860. Ed. Charlotte Mitchell. London: Penguin Books, Ltd., 1996.

Spiritual Discovery Within Complexity

Johnnetta B. Cole

We live in a world where it seems there are no simple problems, a world which calls on its leaders to be poised in the midst of confusion, complexity, and sometimes chaos. I believe that the way one discovers spirituality in such a time is to walk the path of simplicity within this confusion. This path must be one's own, and no one can tell another what the grounding principles should be. Once an individual identifies his or her touchstones, they will see that individual through the most difficult and challenging times. As leaders in such a time, we must be centered and grounded in these principles, for that is what it means to lead, to bring a calm assurance and clear vision when it seems many others are lost in the chaos.

There are three guiding principles that I depend on for decision making. First, I know that I have the responsibility to empower others. That is what lies behind all education. I must help others move toward the fulfillment of their greatest potential. There is no other reason to be an educator. Second, I am called to see the divinity in others; I mean by this each individual's humanity, preciousness, and potential for greatness. Third, I must fulfill these responsibilities without ego investment, for my role is to serve, not to control, or be glorified through the work.

I find that these principles are applicable to each and every issue that confronts me as a leader. All the forces of our lives are related, and the complexities and issues, while intensely challenging at times, can become simplified and unified when we return to our guiding principles. As a leader who is a public intellectual, I recount these guiding principles to myself each and every time I struggle with what I should say, and when and how I should speak out about controversial issues such as the war in Iraq, single sex marriage, and Latina/Latino immigration into the United States. If I do not speak up, how will my students discover their own voices on important but controversial issues? If I remain silent, whose humanity, including my own, will I deny? For any leader the task of speaking up must be about a search for truths, and not some need to pontificate from a soapbox.

I am in the professional position I occupy as a result of many people and many blessings. However, I know that one of the greatest blessings that was given to me is the mindset to respect differences among the world's people for what they are—simply the color of one's skin, or how two people couple, or an individual's gender. Such attributes, I was taught, are never to be used as the basis of judging a person's character. That is my heritage. My mother was a strong, independent, career-minded woman who taught me the principles of feminism by how she behaved far more than by what she said. I am convinced that my father was a protofeminist in the sense that he demonstrated through his actions that he believed in the fundamentals of equality between women and men. In our home, notions of white and male superiority were challenged. I grew up with a loud, unequivocal message that I should get an education because otherwise I might be at the mercy of a man. We were taught that we were smart and could have control over our lives. Sisterhood was a value passed on by my mother and the Black women in my community of her generation who taught me that I must respect all Black women and be sensitive to their economic differences.

My education at Oberlin College exposed me to Jewish, Muslim, and Hindu believers and helped me to value diversity in religious beliefs and practices. Understanding homophobia came much later in my life, when I was confronted in the 1970s with my own heterosexism when a student in one of my classes at the University of Massachusetts in Amherst challenged me.

Recognition of the divinity of others is the starting point for being a servant leader, and while one must do an honest assessment of one's own strengths and weaknesses, it is most important to acknowledge and draw on the talents and assets of others. Everyone deserves respect and compassion and the opportunity to grow into liberation. With the mantle of leadership comes the responsibility of knowing when to be silent, and even when to stand still. Recognizing the amazing gifts of others is one of the most important strengths a leader can have. I stated earlier that my role is to serve without ego investment. Servant leaders are in their positions not for status, power, or the misuse of authority, but to help bring those they are leading toward full empowerment and liberation. Granting the truth that one never knows it all enriches the community beyond measure, and gives others the opportunity to grow into their own genius. The best leadership is the leadership that helps guide others into their own greatest potential.

At its most fundamental level, education is about knowledge, and knowledge is the key to liberation. Slavery and knowledge are not compatible. Every slave master in history has known that. Therefore, because what I do an as educator is to open the door to liberation of the mind and the spirit, education is both mental and spiritual work.

Spiritual leadership starts first with the leader's self exploration. One must be on a personal quest, a lifetime journey of exploration if one is to inspire others to seek liberation. On occasions when I am asked which Christian denomination I am affiliated with I respond that over the course of my lifetime I have been a member of an African Methodist Episcopal Church (AME); I have been an Episcopalian; I have been a member of a United Church of Christ Congregation; and I now worship at and am a member of a United Methodist Church in whose basement, when it was in another location in 1873 as a Methodist Episcopal Church, Bennett College began. As I continue to explore my personal quest for spiritual centeredness, I acknowledge that I am strongly propelled by the belief that my God is too big to belong to any one denomination or religious community.

My guiding principles of empowerment, recognition of divinity in others, and commitment to service I bring to bear on the overall mission of making liberation accessible to others within the community of the academy. For I believe with John W. Gardner, that "it is community and culture that holds the individual in a framework of values and when the framework disintegrates the individual value systems disintegrate" (113). Without commitment to community there is no balance to the narcissism that follows. Without a commitment to community I cannot be true to my mission of empowering others. An authentically spiritual leader must be profoundly connected, first to the community she serves and then to humanity at large. I believe the national disaster of Hurricane Katrina reflected a deep loss of connection and community in our country. By a loss of connection, or a disconnect, I mean separation of oneself from some part of reality. When the intelligence of the heart is disconnected, devalued, and denied, you then have a view of reality that does not include respect for the emotional self. In too many cases, this is what has happened in modern American life. And if you have separated and disregarded your own emotional self, there is only one step from there to a disconnect from others.

When we disengage from the heart, we can justify anything. When all that really matters is that which is material and can be measured, then anything that cannot be counted, including genuine human feeling, and anything that cannot be fully understood by reason or controlled by force is suspect, and feared. There are not many steps from there to the destruction of a sense of community and a breakdown of civil society. When we disregard our humanity, humanity becomes second to material gain; people who are seen as less valuable to this material agenda become invisible and dispensable. The feminine is devalued and women are seen as lesser, as objects of exploitation; nature and the environment are not valued, and no responsibility is taken for their preservation. If you disconnect from everyone who does not look like you, worship like you, couple like you, or agree with you, you can justify any action or lack of action toward "those" people.

All of this is inseparable from what motivates me as a spiritually responsible leader. If one ignores one's full humanity, which by definition involves the heart and its concerns, then no one really counts except you and yours, and your individual agenda. The environment is expendable as long as you are served by its destruction; war is justified if it serves, not the common good, but the good of those who will profit from it; poverty is just an unfortunate consequence of poor folks not pulling themselves up by their bootstraps, even if they have no boots. Programs that do not serve you and yours, but serve the "other" in society can be sacrificed with impunity whether those "other people" are old people, children, or those who are racially, ethnically, or culturally different from you. This breakdown in the social contract results in outrage and anti-social behavior among those who suffer because of the disconnect. They know they do not count in the society. The domino effect of disconnection is overwhelming in a world that is completely interdependent. Through education, we have a wonderful opportunity to heal the disconnect and teach another way to be to the young as well as to ourselves.

Today it is clear that we are faced with the challenge of using all of our creative energies to forge a new way of being in the world. One only has to pick up any publication, or listen to any newscast to be struck by the appalling level of violence, breakdown of systems, and inhumanity that we visit upon each other. If we are to continue life on this planet, we must have a commitment to a new vision and we must have the will to implement this vision. This new way of being rests on admitting that we are all interdependent. There is a beautiful African proverb that captures this reality. It says: "I am because you are. You are because I am." This idea is a central part of my grounding as a spiritual leader for I do believe that our hope is in teaching the youngest of us all, and in finding ways to support their development of a new way to be in the world. There is no higher calling as a leader.

In my view, if a person is to be whole and healthy, there must be a belief in something bigger than oneself, whether or not you call that God. And there must be a recognition that common humanity is just that—common, shared, and communal. Together we are something much bigger than the sum of our parts. That community is a reality that must be acknowledged, or it becomes its own devouring monster. If I do not believe in a God big enough to encompass the entire family of humanity, then I cannot be about affirming that family. And when I make that God exclusive to a certain faith, or I do not take into account those who do not call it God, or call their God by a different name, I allow destructive disconnections to happen.

What is so destructive about believing the center of the universe is your exclusive turf is that you must constantly defend it to the exclusion of your sisters and brothers who happen to look or speak or believe differently, and the more afraid you are of their different expressions of belonging to what is a single human race, the more bigoted and rigid you become. I must honor the way others choose to express their beliefs, and educate with a view toward opening rather than closing minds. Indeed, to insist that one's religious beliefs are the only beliefs that any human being should have will eventually rob one of the most precious possession anyone can have: his or her humanity. My commitment to community and belief in the basic truth that we are all connected is what informs my work in education as well as the world at large. I am more convinced than ever, that we must help all who are in our schools, work places, and the world to create and maintain human connections that transcend differences, and we must foster an understanding of our interdependence and common humanity.

My belief that education is both mental and spiritual work means that I must address the tendency of this generation to disconnect by way of technology. While technology keeps us in touch electronically, it does often separate us from our common humanity, our emotions, and the souls of others. It is important to recognize this as a fact of modern life and to build into our institutions a deliberate balance to the predominance of the machine.

Cell phones can disconnect us from the world around us, from the here and now, and from what we are feeling. Computers can disconnect us from family, or from companions who are in our space but not truly with us; video games and television can disconnect us from everyone NOT on the screen, from those less fortunate than we are, and from present time. All of this technology can disconnect us from what we are feeling, from our thinking process, and from the natural world, but it cannot give us the will to revere and value nature, other people, and ourselves.

As much as we would like to think so, technology cannot fix everything. We had the technology to foresee Katrina and to reinforce the levees. But we lacked the will as a government to do so. It has yet to be proven whether we have the will to bring some measure of justice and restitution to those who were the victims of negligence prior to and following Hurricane Katrina. When areas in the Gulf region are rebuilt, will they once again become the areas of haves and have nots, of White folks in one part of town and people of color in another? Will the evacuees who are poor even have a real chance of continuing their lives in their home city? Clearly, it is not technology that will remedy these ills. It is the will to respond to what is the right thing to do.

How do we go about teaching young people and ourselves to look critically at the technological achievements of our times *and* to measure these achievements against the human needs of all of our sisters and brothers? The abundance of technological "toys" is especially appealing to the young. Adult educators often say it is another world from the one they used to know. With this in mind, it is clear that there is a new challenge for us, and that is to educate the heart in the age of technology.

Although in this culture we may *seem* to be more connected than we have ever been—through cell phones, email, video, ipods, and whatever evolves next week—this is perhaps the most disconnected generation we have ever known. Used wisely, of course, technology is a wonderful thing. However, it seems to have the effect of making us forget some important truths, for example, the basic truth that no man or women is an island unto him- or herself. The instant nature of so much of technology encourages us to act as if there is no past, that there is only here and now and all that lies ahead of us. There is an African proverb that says: "If you don't know where you've come from, you can't know where you're going."

Second, it is also truly critical that we reconnect to nature. Technology can bring you many things fast. But it cannot bring you the relationship to nature that is our biological birthright. If we allow the world around us to become alien because we are constantly plugged into a machine of some kind or another, we may forget that we are, in fact, God's most marvelous natural creations, made from the dust of the stars. For the sake of our spiritual lives, we need to remember where we came from. Not listening to the natural world can result in catastrophe. Not respecting nature is a path to disaster. The world's scientists are in a state of alarm because our government has chosen to drag its feet in response to the certainty that global warming is upon us to our certain detriment. Pollution has resulted in increasingly dangerous levels of damage to the ozone. In spite of growing support from the chemical industry and environmentalists for phasing out several highly toxic substances, new compounds continue to be introduced into global commerce at a rapid rate.

Deforestation, rising sea levels associated with climate change, river engineering, and poor development choices have made us more vulnerable to natural disasters than ever before, and these constitute only the tip of the iceberg when we understand the totality of the problem. We need scientists who will explain how to protect our oceans, and, yes, who can tell us how to repair what we have so carelessly done. But that knowledge, without public policies and laws to do what must be done, will not save our natural and unexplored resources. Without a reverence for nature, little can be done to save us from ourselves. It is not an alarmist statement to say that unless we mend our ways, the time will come when we will not be able to sustain life on our beautiful planet. The very safety of our planet especially requires that our young people re-establish an understanding of the dangers of assaulting the environment.

What a different state our world would be in if we truly acknowledged our related-ness to the natural world and to each other. An expression from Native American lore captures this reality with these words: "With all that is living, I am kin." There is a reason that the Native American phrase "all my relations" refers not just to what is commonly called one's blood kin, but to all living things.

We need one another on this little planet in order to survive. The interrelatedness is unavoidable. We do not have a choice. The food we eat is grown and processed by someone else, probably of another religion; the clothes we wear are made of fabric woven by someone else, probably of another country, and probably of another race; the roof over our heads is constructed by someone else, maybe of another sexual orientation. All of these necessities come from someone else's labor. The more we can honor the connections, the more human we will become and the richer our lives will become. I can think of nothing more important to do as a spiritually grounded leader than to foster and support this truth. As Martin Luther King said: "We are caught in an inescapable network of mutuality, tied in a single garment of destiny. Whatever affects one directly, affects all indirectly" (qtd. in Burrow 240). Reconnecting has the added value of teaching us gratitude that we are not alone. We are all in debt to someone or something for who we are.

The community I support as a leader must be inclusive of diversity, promote caring and compassion, and create shared governance. In this vision there is no room for ego-centered leadership. Servant leaders must model the values they wish to support. Indeed, as the saying goes, you can't lead where you won't go.

The community service that I do with United Way—from the local level initially in Atlanta and now in Greensboro, to serving as the chair of the Board of Trustees of United Way of America (the first person of color to do so) from 2004-2006—has shown me again and again the importance of "bringing everyone to the table" if community problems are to be effectively understood and solved. If the table is not big enough for the diversity of folks in a community to have a seat, then we must build a bigger table.

Finally, I must say that I believe spiritual leadership is a journey, a pilgrimage of perpetual discovery, if you will. It is a personal quest that lasts one's entire life, and promises the privilege of offering the acquired insights, wisdom, courage, and compassion in the interest of others. Richard R. Niebuhr writes, "Pilgrims are persons in motion passing through territories not their own—seeking something we might call completion, or perhaps the word *clarity* will do as well, a goal to which only the spirit's compass points the way" (7). The point is that to attempt to lead without engaging in a quest for personal spiritual development will hardly bring productive results for anyone. And since one of the greatest lessons a leader can teach is that life is a process, not an event, having the courage to stay the course is mighty important.

Like any journey, the journey of leadership is not without its pitfalls. Sometimes we will make mistakes, and sometimes we will go down the wrong paths. But having committed to spiritually grounded leadership we understand that losing our way is part of the pilgrimage, and we will find our way again as long as we are centered in our own truths. My journey as a leader has taught me that there is no difficulty that is not made easier, no chaos that is not made clearer, and no decision that is not made simpler if I stay on my spiritual path. The best leaders follow their hearts as well as their heads, and they never, ever leave their principles behind.

Robin Gray, a First Nation student at Bennett College for Women, sent to me as a gift the Native American Ten Commandments. They are representative of my own guiding principles, and I will close by quoting them:

- The Earth is our Mother; care for Her.
- Honor all your relations.
- Open your heart and soul to the Great Spirit.
- All Life is sacred; treat all beings with respect.
- Take from the earth what is needed and nothing more.
- Do what needs to be done for the good of all.
- Give constant thanks to the Great Spirit for each day.
- Speak the truth but only for the good in others.
- Follow the rhythms of nature.
- Enjoy life's journey, but leave no tracks.

Works Cited

Burrow Jr., Rufus. *God and Human Dignity: The Professionalism, Theology, and Ethics of Dr. Martin Luther King, Jr.* Notre Dame: Notre Dame UP, 2006.

Gardner, John W. *On Leadership.* New York: Free Press, 1990.

Neibuhr, Richard R. "Pioneers and Pilgrims." *Parabola* 9.3 (1984):6-13.

The Dance of a Lifetime: The Transaction of Individual and Community and Work

Sally Z. Hare

Not until we winter into wisdom can we see the dance we have been dancing all our lives, the transaction of Individual and Community and Work. We see what we know. And some things have to be believed to be seen.

The distinguished literacy educator Louise Rosenblatt, in her pioneering work *Making Meaning with Texts*, gives me insight into the word *transaction* and affirms my choice of that word for this dance. In her transactional theory of reading and writing, she explains that she has adopted the term *transaction* from the philosopher John Dewey. The term *interaction*, according to Dewey

> is usually associated with a one-way process in which separate, static things are involved: one predefined unchanging thing acts on another. For example Newtonian physics is interactional: it considers as suitable for scientific experiments only problems that deal with factors that can be held constant. In contrast, in Einstein's physics, the observer as well as the things being studied are taken into account. They are in a reciprocal, transactional relationship, continually changing, shaping and being shaped by one another in relation to changing time and space. (x)

That describes my knowing of the Individual and Community and Work—a lifelong transaction, a dance of mutuality and reciprocity, which is illustrated in the diagram below.

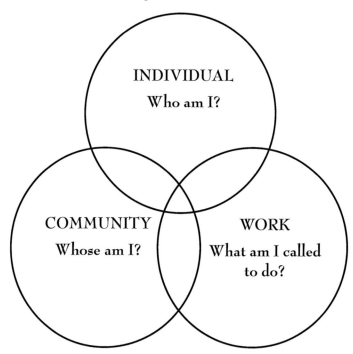

Life is a dance, not a linear uphill battle. It begins as a dance between our role as individual and our role as community member. It's a dance between light and shadow, a dance between simplicity and complexity, a dance between abundance and scarcity. This dance is about embracing paradox, about being in life in a way that is not *either/or* but *both/and*. It's a lifelong dance between who we are and whose we are and what we are here to do, a lifelong dance co-creating our Work in the world, developing our birthright gifts so we can use them in service of the community. Through the process of this lifelong dance, we are constantly constructing and co-constructing the Individual and Community and Work.

I have spent most of my professional life in education looking at communities in classrooms and in schools, in workplaces and on college campuses, deepening my understanding that we humans are communal creatures—and that learning for us is a social action and interaction. Only as I winter into wisdom do I also recognize that we spend our lives in a dance co-creating **who** we are and **whose** we are and our Work in the world, **what** we are called to do. Only with the grace of wintering into wisdom are we able to experience the dance of Self and Community and of "being" our Work in the world. The thirteenth-century Persian mystic and poet Rumi tells us that

> if you forget everything else and not this, there's nothing to worry about, but if you remember everything else and forget this, then you will have done nothing in your life . . . . So human beings come to this world to do particular work. That work is the purpose, and each is specific to the person. (qtd. in Barks 22)

Coleman Barks, in his wonderful translation of Rumi's poetry, gives me my definition for Work: to "let the beauty we love be what we do" (31).

Individual and Community: The Dance Begins

We are born into community. Even before birth, we are interconnected with our mothers, with the environment. Even as we leave the uterine cocoon to move out into the world, we stay attached to our birth mothers with a cord that provides everything we need to live in the outer world. The cutting of the umbilical cord literally forces our first baby steps in the lifelong dance of embracing the paradox of the individual and the community. We come into the world connected, and we immediately enter the tango of separation and attachment, the ballet of letting go and holding on, that distinguishes the seasons of human life. We begin, from our first breath, living in the paradoxical roles of the individual and the community.

Community is fundamental to the learning that is the essence of being human. From early childhood, our first work is developing the sense of trust that is essential to being a healthy member of the community. The psychologist Erik Erikson identifies this vital first stage in his developmental theory of social and emotional development as occurring between birth and age two. Erikson believes that the child, when nurtured and loved, learns trust and security and a sense of optimism in these early years—or becomes mistrustful and insecure without adequate love and nurturing (55-56). The work of the Russian psychologist Lev Vygotsky leaves no doubt that learning is a social, communal act. Learning awakens a variety of internal processes that operate only when the learner is interacting with others (Peterson 3).

Parker Palmer offers insight into the transaction between the Individual and the Community and the Work with his description of individual growth and development as stages towards "life on the Mobius strip"[1] where we continuously co-create our inner and outer worlds (*Hidden Wholeness* 45-49). Palmer says that we come into the world whole, undivided, complete with our birthright gifts. But over the next decade or two, as we move through adolescence and schooling, we too often become deformed. We spend the first half of our lives abandoning our birthright gifts, Palmer writes in *Let Your Life Speak*, or letting others disabuse us of them (12). We learn to separate our authentic selves from the personas we bring forward to receive approval from others, whether parents or teachers or peers. We do so for many reasons, but behind all of them, Parker reminds us, is the ancient motive of self-protection. We lose faith in our gifts, as they move into the shadow, out of our awareness. We lose touch with our essential selves, with what makes us feel most alive. We have a "public face"—and a private one.

As we grow more and more divided, the tension between our roles as individuals and our roles as community members increases, and we feel confusion about our work, our purpose. At some point in adulthood, Palmer recognizes that we start feeling "the consequences

1   The Mobius strip, named for the German mathematician A. F. Mobius, is a one-sided surface made by joining the ends of a rectangle after twisting one end through 180 degrees. (*The Oxford Dictionary and Thesaurus*, Oxford University Press, 1996.)

of living behind a wall: the pain of being disconnected from our own truth" (*Hidden Wholeness* 43-44). Now we may move into another stage, one in which we learn to center ourselves, literally encircling our inner selves with whatever it takes to protect our shy souls, our inner beings, from the world: titles, jokes, jargon, slang, scholarly language, alcohol, overwork. The final stage in Palmer's theory occurs when we make the decision to "live divided no more" (*Hidden Wholeness* 37). In this stage, we determine that nothing anyone else can do to us is worse than what we do to ourselves by not being who we are, by not doing the work we are called to do, by not remembering our birthright gifts and using them in service of the community. Palmer illustrates this stage with the Mobius strip, where one literally can't tell where the outer stops and the inner begins. The individual lives a seamless life, moving effortlessly between her inner world and outer world. Palmer reminds us that there is no "inside" and "outside" on the Mobius strip, that "the two apparent sides keep co-creating the other" (*Hidden Wholeness* 47). The other stages are illusions. "[. . . W]e all live on the Mobius strip all the time: There is no place to hide! We are constantly engaged in a seamless exchange between whatever is 'out there' and whatever is 'in here,' co-creating reality, for better or worse" (*Hidden Wholeness* 47).

Outward Bound to Explore Community

A Kellogg fellowship in the early '90s allowed me to explore the concept of community in different settings—the sense of community in the home and the workplace, in schools and countries, in the state and on the planet. I wanted to better understand how this sense is created. I wanted to expand my own perspective, to better understand leadership and power in the building of community, to better understand the role of leader as facilitator, of power as empowering, of collaboration rather than competition. I hoped to become more "forward-looking," to be more "outward-looking." I wanted to move beyond a hierarchical approach to living and learning to one that is more relational. I see this way of living and learning as more than acquiring new skills, but rather as acquiring an entirely new perspective, a new way of seeing and thinking, a paradigm shift.

My Kellogg fellowship began with Colorado Outward Bound, an experience designed to connect our new group of fellows and create a sense of community. The experience seemed even more appropriate when I learned that the term "outward bound" comes from the blue-and-white flag seamen fly at the start of a journey across the Atlantic, indicating that a ship is leaving safe harbor. I didn't realize until later the deeper significance of the metaphor, holding for me insight into the paradox of the individual and the community in the continuous cycle of leaving and returning home, of letting go and attaching, of moving out and moving in. Through the Kellogg fellowship, I traveled widely, spending time in communities around the globe, from Bali to Greece, from Australia to Mexico. I interviewed leaders in various communities, from a traditional healer in Ubud, wise in the ways of black and white magic, to Mary Robinson, then the first woman to be elected president of Ireland. I also met Parker Palmer—who stretched my thinking about leadership and community. Parker created a space in which I came to understand that community is about emptying and opening, rather than about building and creating. He changed my perception of community from a goal to be achieved to a gift to be received.

The tiny Indonesian island of Bali also managed to turn my worldview upside down. The community is the center of Balinese culture, and communal activities revolve around three temples in each village. Religious beliefs, rituals, and festivals guide the Balinese from birth to death and beyond. They provide a cohesive force within the family and form the basis for community. The sense of community is evident even in the Balinese greeting of "Have you had your rice today?" If the answer is no—then the person shares his or her rice with you. The Balinese care for family members—and take them in if they have no homes, building additional rooms in their family compounds. I found no homeless or starving people in this so-called third-world country.

The Balinese consider their children holy. The younger a person is, the closer her soul to heaven and the purer her spirit. Babies have just come from God, so they are not permitted to touch the impure earth before their first birthday and are carried everywhere. Balinese children are never left alone, nor are they ever physically punished, and rarely are they upset. I entered this world, the arrogant "first-world" American with a PhD in education, specializing in early childhood, thinking I was the expert. And I expected to find spoiled children. I found just the opposite. The Balinese children are calm, friendly, well adjusted, open, with no fear of strangers. They appear to be "community gifted," with a strong sense of belonging and a way of extending welcome that seems innate. They care for each other— and are affectionate and compassionate.

Mothers massage their babies for at least 40 minutes several times a day until they are three or four years old. Not only does this provide a warm bond between mother and child, but the children are incredibly graceful. Fathers and mothers, as well as brothers and sisters, share childcare responsibilities. It is not unusual to see a man with a young child, caring for her while he sells goods from his market stand. Mothers often have babies strapped on their backs as they wash clothes in a nearby river. And older children often walk hand in hand with younger ones in the green fields and quiet streets.

The Balinese also consider their old people to be holy. Old people are getting ready to return to God as they winter into wisdom. There are no nursing homes or isolation for these elders. Rather, they are vital members of the community, serving as healers and teachers, living within the family compounds. I am particularly struck by one hut that is part of each family compound—the home of the elder women, who usually outlive their husbands. This space is considered holy ground, and others do not enter, with one exception. Young girls, during the week of their first menstruation, spend time in the sacred space with the elder women, listening to stories and being welcomed into womanhood. I could not help but contrast that with the isolating experience of American middle-school girls when they start their periods.

Community is very intertwined with spirituality in the Balinese culture, a difficult concept for this American to grasp. My Balinese teachers gently chided me for my either/or way of looking at the world. "You Americans think it has to be either good or evil," an elderly Balinese woman said to me. "It's not that way at all. It has to be both. We wouldn't have good if there were no evil. It's all about balance."

I began my Kellogg fellowship with the goal of becoming more outward looking. I soon realized that I also have to look inward. And in case I forget, life continues to remind me that it's not *either/or*, but *both/and*. The terrorist bombing in Bali in October 2002, has affected the gentle nation and hurt the tourism that is the base of its economy. A sign at my local airport this month tells me the airport in Denpasar, Bali's capital, is considered unsafe by my government. The people of Kuta, the location of the bombing, have erected a shrine at the site and still bring flowers daily. A sign at the memorial, reported recently on the Internet by a tourist, reads: "[D]on't let us live with the angriness, the sadness and sorrow . . . . God please make us stronger" (Mackenzie np).

Dancing in the Field

We speak of community as if it exists outside of the individual— but in fact, it is an integral part of the self. Our English language has no adequate words for describing the wholeness, the integrated form that is the self and the community, the inner and the outer. Palmer intimates the connectedness, the oneness, when he writes that community begins in the recesses of the human heart (*Courage to Teach*). That resonates with me, but I find myself asking the old chicken and the egg question of which comes first, knowing that the human heart also begins in community, literally connected through an umbilical cord.

A recent report from the national Commission on Children at Risk, an independent, jointly sponsored initiative of the YMCA of the USA, Dartmouth Medical School, and the Institute for American Values, says we are "hardwired to connect" (1). The group of 33 children's doctors, research scientists, and mental health and youth service professionals, headed by principal investigator Dr. Kathleen Kovner Kline of Dartmouth Medical School, concludes "that the mechanisms by which children become attached to others are biologically primed and can be discerned in the structure of the brain" (14). So community begins in the human brain as well. And the current research in early childhood brain development shows that the human brain begins in community. More than half of brain development occurs in the first two years of life, requiring nurturing, loving connections with adults. There is a four-year critical period from conception until about the third birthday during which the child is learning language and the other physical and social and emotional skills to be a competent community member. Perhaps we should speak of community acquisition and community readiness in early childhood as we speak of language acquisition and reading readiness. Then we might recognize and value parents and teachers of young children as teachers of the dance of community.

The linguist Noam Chomsky tells us that we come into the world with a disposition for language. Chomsky says that children are born with a knowledge of the principles of the grammatical structure of all languages, and this inborn knowledge explains the success and speed with which they learn language. Knowing a language means being able to produce an infinite number of sentences never spoken before and to understand sentences never heard before, an ability Chomsky names the "creative aspect" of language (6). Clearly we also come into the world with a disposition for community, and we also have a "creative aspect" for community, an ability to connect with others we have never seen before. We recognize when a child knows language, and we honor that it is a process, but do we recognize when the youngster knows community and value *that* process? We claim with excitement that the two-year-old is talking. Do we need a verb to express similar excitement when the child is "communitying"?

Archbishop Desmond Tutu says we have no English word for this way of being. "In Africa we have a word, *ubuntu*, which is difficult to render in Western languages. It speaks about the essence of being human: that my humanity is caught up in your humanity because we say a person is a person through other persons. I am a person because I belong. The same is true for you. The solitary human being is a contradiction in terms" (xiii).

Mark Nepo uses the Sanskrit word *akasha*, referring to a collective presence and memory among human beings. "In the west, we tend to ignore this," Nepo writes in *Facing the Lion, Being the Lion: Finding Inner Courage Where it Lives*, "insisting we are separate and unattached. Yet there is molecular and biological evidence of our Oneness and how our very presence influences each other, how being influences being" (170).

Once again I turn to the thirteenth-century poet Rumi for the best words to describe what I am coming to know, that field in which we dance between Individual and the Community and Work:

> Out beyond ideas of wrong-doing and right-doing
> there is a field.
> I'll meet you there.
>
> When the soul lies down in that grass
> the world is too full to talk about
>
> Ideas, language, even the phrase
>   each other
>   doesn't make any sense. (qtd. in Barks 98)

Of Definitions and Complex Choreography

Community is. We exist in community. Community exists in us. We can't exist without community. We need the love and care and attention of others to thrive, even to survive. Rene Spitz's 1940s study of institutionalized orphans has shown these babies and young children literally turn their faces to the wall and die although their physical needs for food and shelter have been met and they have no discernable problems. With a bare minimum of human contact and affection, these babies suffer devastatingly. An enormous number do not even survive to two years of age. Those who do survive are physically stunted, highly prone to infection, and severely retarded, both cognitively and emotionally. By three years of age, most are still unable to walk or talk, and they are withdrawn and apathetic (Spitz 402).

We need relationships with others; we need love; we need touch; we need community. We are communal creatures. We are community. Yet we have been defining community as something outside of us, something separate.

Creation myths offer human attempts in every culture, in every time, to explain community, to reduce it to its lowest common denominator, to make it something around which we can wrap our hands. According to researchers Eugene d'Aquili and Andrew Newburg, human beings appear to have "no choice but to construct myths . . . to explain their world" (154). In the Balinese myth of creation, God fashions figures of clay, but leaves them in the oven too long, and they are an over-baked black. With the next batch, perhaps overly cautious, God doesn't leave the figures in long enough, and they are an underdone white. The last batch of people is just right, a golden brown, and they are the Balinese.

In another sense, the sciences (particularly biology, physics, psychology, sociology) are other human attempts to explain, to know, to find meaning, to reduce the idea of community to a definition, an explanation. Autopoiesis, the term coined by the

Chilean biologists Humberto Maturana and Francisco Varela, from the Greek roots meaning self (*auto*) and making (*poiein*, as in "poetry"), refers to life's continuous production of itself (qtd. in Margulis and Sagan 18). Lynn Margulis is very intentional in the inclusion of humans when she postulates that all of Earth is community, a living system, of which we humans are a part. Her theory of symbiogenesis emphasizes the importance of cooperation over the Darwinian tradition of competition, of community as the essence of all life. "We are coming to realize that we are part of a global holarchy[2] that transcends our individual skins and even humanity as a whole" (18). The mathematical cosmologist Brian Swimme sees community as the solution to the crisis of mass extinction he feels we are facing today. He says we need to

> reinvent ourselves, at the species level, in a way that enables us to live with mutually enhancing relationships . . . . Not just with humans but with all beings—so that our activities actually enhance the world. At the present time, our interactions degrade everything . . . . What's necessary is for us to understand that, really, at the root of things is community. At the deepest level, that's the center of things. We come out of community. So how then can we organize our economics so that it's based on community, not accumulation? And how can we organize our religion to teach us about community? And when I say "community," I mean the whole earth community. That's the ultimate sacred domain—the earth community. (qtd. in Bridle np)

Perhaps it's difficult to comprehend or even recognize community when we are community. Maybe it helps to get out and look back, as

2   The word *holarchy* was coined by Arthur Koestler (1905-1983) to mean the coexistence of small beings in larger wholes. Koestler's coinage is free of implications of "hierarchical" or "higher" or that one of the constituents in the holarchy is somehow controlling the others (Margulis and Sagan, 1995, p. 17).

Eugene A. Cernan, an astronaut on both the Gemini and Apollo
lunar missions, did:

> When you are in Earth orbit looking down you see
> lakes, rivers, peninsulas . . . . You quickly fly over
> changes in topography, like the snow-covered
> mountains or deserts or tropical belts . . . . You pass
> through a sunrise and sunset every ninety minutes.
> When you leave Earth orbit, you can see from pole
> to pole without even turning your head . . . . You
> literally see North and South America go around the
> corner as Earth turns on an axis you can't see and
> then miraculously Australia, then Asia, then all of
> America comes to replace them . . . . You ask yourself,
> where am I in space and time? You watch the sun set
> over America and rise again over Australia. You look
> back "home" . . . and don't see the barriers of color,
> religion, and politics that divide up the world. (qtd. in
> Margulis and Sagan 18)

The definitions of community are embedded in culture and
context, in time and place. The meaning is dynamic, constantly
changing. The concept is neither linear nor static, evident even in its
Latin roots. The origin of the word "community" comes from the Latin
munus, which changed in meaning over time from "duty" to "service"
to "gift" to "public showing." *Munus* is combined with the Latin *cum*,
"with" or "among each other" or "in the company of" or "on the side
of," suggesting meaning shifts even in Roman times from "those
in whose company one serves" to "those among whom one gives" to
"those with whom one publicly sides." The Latin word then evolved to
communis, meaning common, and *communion*, to strengthen or fortify
on all sides, and later meaning mutual participation.

Mastering the lifelong dance of community means acknowledging
the complex choreography, including definitions that change over time
and place. The current *Oxford English Dictionary* (*OED*) ignores the
complicated history, simplifying it to the word "community" deriving

from the Latin root, *commun, communis,* meaning common. The same root is the base of the word "communicate": to share understanding, to have understanding in common. "Communion," another word from the same root, means a sharing in common. A community, according to the *OED,* is a group of people or of nations unified by having something in common.

The *OED's* simplification reminds me of a favorite quote, attributed to Chief Justice Oliver Wendell Holmes: "I wouldn't give a fig for the simplicity that lies this side of complexity, but I would give my life for the simplicity that lies on the other side of complexity" (*Quoteopia!*). So for that simplicity on the other side of complexity, I suggest we look again at the word "community": *com* (with) + *unity* (oneness). Nepo reminds us of the "molecular and biological evidence of our Oneness" (170). The word "comm<u>unity</u>" contains "unity." And that is the foundation for the dance.

Expanding the Dance

Even with the many creation myths and scientific definitions, I find very little in the literature that addresses the use of the word "community" as a space where the shy soul might make an appearance, what Parker Palmer calls a circle of trust (*A Hidden Wholeness* 59). In a recent interview, Palmer expresses poignantly the "lack of external forms of community that invite inner journeys." Palmer speaks to the need for us to be receptive to this kind of community in our culture rather than our current emphasis on making such community. "There is still so much emphasis on making everything. We are so locked into the manufacturing mindset" (2006).

We have to be intentional about expanding the dance to include the inner self as well as the outer world. We have to be open to taking the inner journey necessary to hearing our calling, as well as the outer journey that prepares us to respond to our vocation, our work in the world. The Individual and the Community and the Work are clearly not a matter of either/or, but rather, a continual co-creation. I am experiencing in my current work, in circles of trust, some transaction of community and individual transformation. Working nationally through the Center for Courage and Renewal (www.couragerenewal. org) and with college presidents at the invitation of Dr. Betty Siegel, I am aware of the reciprocity of the Individual and the Community and the Work in a new way.

I see, too, the significance of solitude in community. There is a connectedness among individuals, an unseen but nevertheless real and present relatedness. Our connectedness deepens in this seemingly counterintuitive way, when we are together in trustworthy spaces that allow us to be who we are, spaces in the natural world with time for reflection and for the intentional slowing of the pace of our lives, spaces of communal silence in which we "be" together and literally hear our own hearts.

I want to be intentional in naming this dance of connectedness. Yes, community has many meanings: a state of being, a skill, an acquired habit, a sense of belonging, a physical address, a religious or national affiliation, a genetic condition, a learned behavior, a stage of development, an aesthetic experience, Oneness. Now, as I see this lifelong dance, I want to expand my definition to include community as space in which humans exist and develop and thrive and change. Community is a space in which the soul can show up. Community is space in which we are pushed beyond our comfort zone, a paradoxical space of boundaries and hospitality in which we can grow and stretch and transform. Community is a space in which we name and claim who we are and whose we are and our work in the world.

Picking Up the Beat

I'm adding dance steps and complexity to this lifelong dance. Maybe the beat has been a bit too slow! I find this dance is moving me to a way of knowing community that is both inner and outer. Remembering Palmer's image of the Mobius strip, I see that our inner selves are always engaged in a seamless interchange with that which is "outside" of us, always co-creating community for better or for worse—exactly as community is co-creating us. As I participate in the reciprocity and mutuality of this dance, I am also co-creating my work, living into my vocation. This continually changing choreography takes me from the position of community as something to be created "out there," external to the individual, a perception of a whole of which the individual is a part, through more complex dance steps to the place of community within the individual, not only confined to the body but also our inner experience of the world, to this seemingly new dance in which community is both inner and outer, is not only an entity of which the individual is part, but a holarchy.

Thomas Merton writes in "Hagia Sophia": "There is in all things visible an invisible fecundity, a dimmed light, a meek namelessness, a hidden wholeness" (506). Parker Palmer says a circle of trust is the space that invites this hidden wholeness to come forth:

> Here is one way to understand the relationships in a circle of trust: they combine unconditional love, or regard, with hopeful expectancy, creating a space that both safeguards and encourages the inner journey. In such a space, we are freed to hear our own truth, touch what brings us joy, become self-critical about our faults, and take risky steps toward change. (*Hidden Wholeness* 72-87)

I know Merton's *"mysterious Unity and Integrity"* (506; Merton's italics) as the transaction of Individual and Community and Work, the dance of a lifetime that is most likely to happen, with grace and with ease, in Palmer's *circle of trust.*

Wintering into Wisdom: A Transactional Theory of Community

Community seems to be the solution for everything wrong in our world today. The breakdown of community is cited as the cause for everything from children murdering each other in schools to racism and ethnocentrism to drug overdoses to the high rates of suicide. The disappearance of community gets the blame for why we are destroying the planet—and it is Brian Swimme's solution for what he calls the crisis of "mass extinction" (qtd. in Bridle np).

Robert Putnam's *Bowling Alone* has become a national bestseller, as we search for ways to understand social change in the United States and the growing sense of disconnectedness and isolation that led to the Columbine shootings and the Oklahoma City bombing. Putnam's detailed graphs and tables point to his belief that we are looking for ways to create or re-create social capital as the antidote for the so-called loss of community. I say "so-called" because I don't believe we lose community any more than I believe we can create it. Humans can't exist without community. If we've lost anything, it's our own hearts—and our own capacity to know what's all around us, to hear our own inner selves, our spirits. We've lost our ability to know community, to recognize the dance.

Community begins at home. Our parents are our first dance teachers. Relationship and communication skills, so essential to community, start, for better and for worse, in the home. Community development has to begin within the individual, as each person reclaims his or her identity and integrity and remembers what it means to know community. And we learn those first dance steps, the basis for community development, at home.

T. S. Eliot's words offer insight into why we can't see this dance that we have been dancing all our lives until we are able to winter into wisdom:

> We shall not cease from exploration
> > and the end of all our exploring
> Will be to arrive where we started
> > and know the place for the first time. (39-42)

Some things have to be believed to be seen. We see what we know. Yes, it takes the grace of wintering into wisdom to see the dance of a lifetime, the transaction of Individual and Community and Work.

Works Cited

Barks, Coleman. *The Illuminated Rumi*. New York: Broadway Books, 1997.

Bridle, Susan. "Comprehensive Compassion: An Interview with Brian Swimme." *What Is Enlightenment?* Ed. Carter Phipps. 19 (2001) *What is Enlightenment Magazine*. 19 (2006). EnlighteNext, Inc. 22 Sept. 2006 <http://www.wie.org/j19/swimme.asp?page=2>.

Chomsky, Noam. *Syntactic Structures*. Ossining, NY: Walter de Gruyter, 2002.

Commission On Children At Risk. *Hardwired to Connect: The New Scientific Case for Authoritative Communities*. New York: Institute for American Values, 2003.

D'Aquili, Eugene D. and Andrew B. Newberg. *The Mystical Mind: Probing the Biology of Religious Experience (Theology and the Sciences)*. Minneapolis: Augsburg Fortress, 1999.

Eliot, T.S. "The Dry Salvages." *Four Quartets*. Orlando: Harvest-Harcourt Brace, 1943. 35-48.

Erikson, Erik. *Identity and the Life Cycle*. 1980. New York: W.W. Norton & Co., 1980.

MacKenzie, Lee. "Bali After the Bomb." *The Batik Butik: Exclusive Handmade Rayon Batik Fabrics from Bali*. 24 July 2006 <http://www.batikbutik.com/bali_insight.htm>.

Margulis, Lynn and Dorian Sagan. *What is Life?* Simon & Schuster, 1995.

Merton, Thomas. *Thomas Merton Reader*. Ed. Thomas P. McDonnell. New York: Double Day, 1989.

Nepo, Mark. *Facing the Lion, Being the Lion: Finding Inner Courage Where It Lives*. San Francisco: Red Wheel Conari, 2007.

Oxford Dictionary and Thesaurus. Oxford UP, 1996.

Palmer, Parker J. *A Hidden Wholeness: The Journey Toward an Undivided Life*. San Francisco: Jossey-Bass, 2004.

---.*Let Your Life Speak*. San Francisco: Jossey-Bass, 2000.

---.*The Courage to Teach*. San Francisco: Jossey-Bass, 1998.

Palmer, Parker J. Telephone interview. 2006.

Peterson, Ralph. *Life in a Crowded Place: Making a Learning Community*. Portsmouth: Heinemann, 1992.

Putnam, Robert D. *Bowling Alone: The Collapse and Revival of American Community*. New York: Simon & Schuster, 2000.

Quoteopia! The Land of Famous Quotations. 2005. 16 March 2007 http://www.quoteopia.com/.

Rosenblatt, Louise. *Making Meaning with Texts: Selected Essays*. Portsmouth: Heinemann, 2005.

Spitz, Rene A. *Rene A. Spitz: Dialogues from Infancy: Selected Papers*. Ed. Robert N. Ende. New York: International Universities Press, 1983.

Tutu, Desmond. Foreword. *Exploring Forgiveness*. Ed. Robert D. Enright and Joanna North. Madison: University of Wisconsin Press, 1998. xiii-xiv.

Vygotsky, L. S. *Mind in Society*. Eds. M. Cole, V. John-Steiner, S. Scribner, and E. Soubermna. Cambridge: Harvard UP, 1978.

Always Remember, Never Forget

Johnny Isakson

The older I get, the more I realize that every success I've had or accomplishment I've achieved has been because of what I learned from others and what others have done for me. Whether as teachers, scout leaders, friends or associates, a lot of people help others get where they're going.

Sometimes one moment in time can put everything in perspective, providing that focus on what others have done to help me achieve.

Such a moment took place for me at the American cemetery in the Netherlands. As a member of the United States Senate and the Veterans Affairs Committee, I traveled to Europe to visit the American cemeteries and participate in Memorial Day ceremonies. It was a responsibility, and once I arrived I realized what a great privilege it was as well. My moment in time came about eleven o'clock in the morning. I was walking between the rows of white crosses and Stars of David, touched by the tremendous sacrifice so many Americans had made to rid Europe and the world of Hitler. I stopped at grave #10 on row 8 in plot G of the American cemetery in the Netherlands. On the white marble cross was etched the name "Roy C. Miller, Private." The date of death, 12/28/44, the day Roy Miller took his last breath was the day I drew my first.

At that moment, I recognized so vividly that someone I never knew sacrificed his life so that I, someone Roy Miller would never know, could enjoy mine. Such a moment in time grants an unbelievable perspective, imposes an intense sorrow, and brings a tear.

I'm not sure how many minutes I stood at that grave, nor can I count the number of thoughts that rushed through my mind, but when I turned and walked away after saying a brief prayer, I realized how much I owed—how much we all owe—to so many we will never know but must always remember.

The New Testament of the Bible in the Book of John, Chapter 15, Verse 13 says, "Greater love has no man than this, that a man lay down his life for his friends." In return for that love we must never forget the sacrifice.

Perspective

I never learned exactly how Private Roy Miller died on December 28, 1944, but he wasn't alone. As I walked the cemetery that day I found at least eight other markers with the same date. So on the day that I was born, at least nine Americans died on soil so far away so that my life would have the hope and the promise of freedom.

In December of 1944 the Allied Forces were driving Hitler out of northern Europe back into Germany. After the success of Normandy came the Battle of the Bulge, and ultimately the Allied Forces' push into Germany. On that day when I visited Roy Miller's grave, I participated in the Memorial Day ceremony. Here it was, the year 2006—62 years after Roy Miller died and the Allies invaded Normandy.

Sixty-two years later, yet 7,000 Dutch came to our memorial ceremony on their soil. The Royal Dutch Men's Chorus sang, "God Bless America," and I cried. At the conclusion of the ceremony, the Royal Dutch Army flew above our heads in American F-16 aircraft in the Missing Man formation. Seventy-two vividly beautiful wreaths had been laid in memory of the Americans who died. They had been placed by everyone from Girl Scouts and Boy Scouts in Holland, to survivors of those who had sacrificed and died, to Dutch citizens who just came to pay tribute to those who died so that they could live.

I thought to myself, "I wonder how many times in America we let Memorial Day go by and never stop or pause to think about

how important it really was what these brave men and women did."
Somehow I wish I could transfer that moment in time and its emotion
and all that I had seen to everyone I come in contact with. Maybe this
article, this writing, this attempt is my way of doing that.

I worry so much sometimes that the last of that great generation
of Americans who fought and sacrificed in World War II is already
passing away. Already their achievements are parts of history books,
with many people never encountering a veteran of that era or an
experience like mine. But then, that moment in time at Roy Miller's
grave, which did bring a great perspective to me, reminded me also
that there are many Roy Millers and there have been many wars and
there will be in the future. It is the legacy of "service above self,"
"God and Country," and "core values" that we have to remember, for
that is what led these brave men and women to battle.

When I think about Roy Miller, not only do I think about what
his sacrifice meant to me and millions of freedom-loving citizens
around the world, but I also shudder to think what wouldn't have
happened if it hadn't been for Roy Miller and those thousands of
Americans like him who sacrificed for freedom and liberty.

Just think of the consequences of not confronting an Adolph
Hitler. In my lifetime alone, had Hitler not been confronted—had
he ultimately prevailed—there never would have been a Civil Rights
Movement in America or a Martin Luther King, Jr.; there would be
no Jews alive today and no state of Israel. "God" would have been
purged from our vocabulary and, ultimately, love purged from our
hearts.

What a frightening thought—what a wonderful gift Roy Miller
and others like him gave to us and all the world. Because he died,
Martin Luther King could live. And because both of them died
for a cause greater than themselves, all of us live in a world that's
better, and free.

That moment in time also caused me to think of others—others
whom I did know—others who sacrificed and died, and others about
whom I would like to share.

Reality

Standing over Roy Miller's grave in the Netherlands brought back another memory—a 39-year-old memory—a memory that dated back to March 1967.

I had just met the lady I would marry. I had just returned from basic training in the National Guard and begun to get my feet on the ground after graduating from college—I had just begun to look to the future when the phone call came. They told me that Jack Cox had died.

At the University of Georgia as a member of the SAE Fraternity, I had a lot of friends, but none of them better than Jack Cox, Alex Crumbley, and Pierre Howard. Jack Cox was a 6 foot 2, 225-pound teddy bear. He was the nicest guy I ever knew—the happiest person I'd ever been around. Almost every night during the week at about 10 o'clock, after studying, Jack, Alex, Pierre, and I, would go to the Key to America Motel Coffee Shop behind the fraternity house and drink coffee and eat pecan pie. We all talked about what we were going to do when we left college. We shared our dreams, our hopes, and our aspirations.

We would always kid Jack about being so big and so strong, yet so nice—in fact, I worried that we may have kidded him too much because when our buddy Jack graduated from the University, he announced to us all that he was joining the Marines, going to Officer Candidate School (OCS), and going to fight for his country in Viet Nam. Jack proved himself to be nice but tough. He graduated from OCS, became a commissioned officer, and went to Viet Nam. We communicated by mail whenever we could, and Alex and Pierre and I always called his mom and dad, Emily and Sidney, in Waynesboro just to see how they were doing. When the phone call came to tell us that Jack had died, we instinctively got in our cars, drove to Waynesboro, and waited with his parents for Jack to arrive home for the last time.

I felt guilty, and although we never talked about it, mostly everyone my age who didn't go to Viet Nam felt guilty, especially when one of their own, one so close, one so young, had died. We spent a week with Jack's folks, and three of those days Jack was with us, lying in state in the home he grew up in on Liberty Street in Waynesboro. Everyone in Burke County came to pay their respects. We sat around and told "Jack Cox" stories and laughed and cried together, dreading the day that was to come when we put Jack to rest in his beloved Burke County.

Reality is that indelible impression that is made upon one's mind by an event or a person. Standing on that hillside, listening to that 21-gun salute, and hearing "Taps" played as your best friend is lowered to his final resting place is a painful reality, and the pain never goes away. It hasn't for me, and I know it hasn't for Emily, and I know as long as Sidney lived it didn't go away for him. But there's something else that doesn't go away equally, and that's the pride of what they did—the sacrifice they gave—the ultimate sacrifice; and they gave it willingly, and they gave it knowingly, and they gave it for me.

Roy Miller's cross in the American cemetery in the Netherlands got my attention and gave me perspective and reminded me of my friend Jack Cox, and that gave me reality.

Reflection

Not long after my visit to the American cemetery in the Netherlands, I attended a "welcome home" ceremony for the 48th Brigade of the Georgia National Guard. The ceremony was held in Monroe, Georgia, on a beautiful, hot Saturday afternoon.

That's the day that I met Robert Stokely. That's the day he gave me Sergeant Mike Stokely's dog tag, which stays in my pocket every day in the United States Senate.

Like Roy Miller, I never met Mike Stokely—but like Roy Miller's sacrifice in the Netherlands in 1944, Mike Stokely's death in Iraq in August of 2005 made a difference in my life. He made the ultimate sacrifice just as Roy Miller had and just as Jack Cox had.

"So we go full circle," I thought. Roy Miller was a member of America's Greatest Generation and he fought and he died so Europe could be free from the tyranny of Nazi Germany. Then Jack Cox, the son of a later generation, volunteered and went to another war in another time in another place, and made the ultimate sacrifice. And here is Mike Stokely, a son of Jack Cox's generation who gave his life in Iraq. In reflection it becomes quite clear—every generation has its conflict, and so far all of us in America, every generation, has had its heroes: Roy Miller, Jack Cox, Mike Stokely.

Now I have children of my own and they have children of their own, and the rest of my life and my future is tied up in loving my children and grandchildren, hoping for them all the opportunity that I have had. I hope their generation has heroes like mine did in Jack Cox, and like my Dad's did in Roy Miller, and like my children do today in Mike Stokely.

I worry that the day might come that too many Americans forget why we're able to do all we're able to do—why we enjoy this freedom and prosperity. I worry that the day might come that the Battles of Normandy and Saigon and Baghdad are just chapters in a history book, and not indelible lessons etched in our minds, indelible because we're reminded of those who sacrificed and paid the ultimate price so that we might live.

As I write this piece and share these thoughts, I deeply hope that it spurs someone else to visit an American cemetery, or say thanks to an American soldier, or volunteer in some way to support this great country we have. But just writing a piece is not enough—we have to talk about our patriotism and we have to live it. I'm thankful I had my moment in time at the grave of Roy Miller, and I hope that sometime in their lives all Americans can have a similar moment in time so that they can gain a perspective, be shocked into reality, and reflect on what a wonderful country this is and on those who gave us a chance to experience it and to love it.

Finding Balance: An Integration of Core Values in All Areas of Life

Nancy S. King

As I reflect back over a 30-year career in higher education, I am struck by how interrelated the various facets of my life have become. More often than I would have liked, however, managing multiple roles over the years made me feel that my life was fragmented rather than a seamless whole. I am reminded of an illustration frequently used by Dr. Betty L. Siegel, Kennesaw State University's president for 25 years, of juggling "rubber balls and glass balls" and of the importance of balance in one's life. During her long tenure as KSU's president, I have heard Dr. Siegel speak eloquently of the value—indeed the critical need—of achieving that balance and of focusing on the "glass balls," which symbolize the priorities that should require our most careful attention, as opposed to the "rubber balls" that bounce back when they are dropped. While this issue is certainly not unique to women, I do believe that many of us struggle with tending the fragile priorities of life and reaching that "balance point" that allows us to find meaning and common purpose in the many roles we play— mother, spouse, partner, friend, employee.

When I was younger, my life did indeed feel more segmented. The basic "divisions" consisted of my personal life—centered on family, friends and social events—and my professional life at Kennesaw State University and in a number of professional associations. My involvement in a church community served as my spiritual base. For the most part, I felt that these areas of life were clearly separate. I knew I had to make time to give attention to each of them in order to reach the "balance" that Dr. Siegel spoke of so often. Looking back, however, I realize that I rarely saw these various "sections" of life as an integrated whole. In all honesty, I also must admit that more often than not my juggling of the glass and rubber balls became out of synch and I ended up breaking fragile areas of my life and devoting far too much attention to things that are correctly described as "rubber balls."

A huge amount of my time has been and continues to be spent in the workplace. For that reason it is essential that I find a sense of meaning and purpose in my professional life. It is not an overstatement to say that our work should nourish our souls as surely as it pays the bills. Far too often, though, a large portion of our days degenerates into a system of repetitive activities and routine tasks that can dull our creativity and numb our spirits. In addition, the workplace is far too often marked by pettiness, backbiting, gossip, and a scrambling to get ahead that deadens our souls. In the process we lose touch with the core values that define who we are as spiritual beings, and as a result we lose our sense of balance. In a chapter titled "The Workplace as Spiritual Haven" in *When the Canary Stops Singing: Women's Perspectives on Transforming Business*, Kim McMillen quotes the Trappist monk Thomas Merton, who observed that "the greatest human temptation is to settle for too little" (116). McMillen feels that for many of us work has become "petty and small" and fails to nourish our souls (116). She argues that "spiritual pioneers" in the workplace can find meaning in their work that dovetails with their most deeply cherished belief systems and privately held values. Clearly, it is not desirable—in fact, it is highly detrimental—to leave spirituality out of one's professional life.

Perhaps one of the rewards of aging is that despite memory that sometimes fails us and eyesight that is clearly diminished, our vision of what matters most in a balanced life becomes much sharper as we mature. There was a time when I allowed "busyness" to overwhelm me to the point that I could not distinguish the rubber balls from the glass, much less focus on the meaning and purpose that should bind together the various segments of my life. Concentrating obsessively on my "to-do list" rather than on the purpose of these isolated tasks and their relation to my inner core often led me to a sense of fragmentation. With aging, however, I have come to see much more clearly those things on my lists (and, yes, I continue to be a list-maker) that deserve my full attention because they reflect my true purpose and those that can be dropped with little or no harm.

Reflecting on what I have learned about balance in life, I realize that gradually, without my even being aware that this shift was occurring, I have become far more sensitive to the connections among the various roles I play, and the walls that separate the compartments of my life have slowly crumbled. I am now far more aware of the core values that permeate all of the areas—personal, professional, and spiritual— that were kept more segmented in my past. In truth, the multiple roles that I play as mother, grandmother, university administrator, member of the higher education community, Sunday school teacher and church member, book club facilitator, and community volunteer are all connected by some very important common threads. In each of my roles these core values, or "threads," weave the various parts of my life into a single identity that makes me who I am in sum. In my most reflective moments, I have come to see that there are four dominant threads woven throughout the fabric of my life. It is when I am keenly aware of these core values and the way they are reflected in all of my roles that I feel most balanced and fulfilled.

Without question the foundation for my life is my spiritual belief system. Increasingly, it is my Christian faith and belief in the higher power that guides me in this life and who will lead me into the life to come that informs all of my roles. Indeed, my Christian values can be said to be the basic guide for my approach to three essential elements: relationships, community, and service. First, my relationship with Christ, whom I believe reveals the face of God for humanity, is deeply embedded in my interactions with family and friends, work colleagues, professional associates, and students. Attempting to live the Christian life changes the way I view those with whom I interact and form relationships. I am encouraged to see each one as a child of God, created in His image and holding great value and potential. This view also influences how I approach conflict, an inevitable part of life; and it has taught me the healing power of forgiveness and the restoration of estranged relationships. Granted, this approach is an ongoing process; I'm not there yet. Far too frequently I'm quick to judge others, to devalue them by my actions and attitudes, and to harbor anger and a refusal to forgive. But because of my faith, I continue striving to see my fellow human beings' worth through God's eyes rather than my own and to extend to them the same grace God has given me. Certainly this effort has made an enormous difference in how I deal with challenging colleagues and with students and others who may be described as "difficult."

My spiritual beliefs also affect my attitude toward the community. Over the years I have developed a growing awareness of the importance of a sense of community. I do not believe that God created us to live in isolation. Rather, He intends that we find our place with others within the community. Henri Nouwen wisely observes that

> Life is full of gains and losses, joys and sorrow . . . but we do not have to live it alone. We want to drink our cup together and thus celebrate the truth that the wounds of our individual lives, which seem intolerable when lived alone, become sources of healing when we live them as part of a fellowship of mutual care. (124)

I am a member of many communities: a family that continues to expand with the addition of in-law children and grandchildren, the KSU community and the wider higher education community through professional associations like the National Academic Advising Association (NACADA), my church and local community groups such as my book club, and the global community through travel and contact with international students. One of the primary values of interaction with these various communities is that they extend my network of relationships. As a result, my life is richer and far more meaningful and interesting than a life lived in isolation.

Two of Dr. Siegel's most frequent quotations come to mind when I think about the importance of community. Many is the time I've heard her say that "community is not a place; it's what's taking place." Perhaps she is best known for her reference to Alex Haley's "turtle on the fencepost." At this stage in my life, I agree wholeheartedly that like turtles on fenceposts, we never "get there by ourselves." I have had many mentors and guides who have helped lift me up through the years, and I am reminded of them every time I hear Dr. Siegel's turtle analogy. Another of my educational heroes, Ernest Boyer, wisely observed that there are "two great traditions of individuality and community in higher education. Colleges . . . should help students become independent, self-reliant human beings, yet also they should give priority to community" (296). Boyer goes on to say that in implementing these two priorities "a balance must be struck" (296). Likewise I have found in my own life that I must continually strike the correct balance between active participation in the community and times of drawing within my own personal self for reflection and meditation on the meaning and purpose of my life.

Clearly, my Christian beliefs and my heroes in higher education have also shaped my views toward service. For me, Christ is the ultimate example of the servant-leader. In John's gospel, following the account of Jesus washing his disciples' feet, we hear Christ saying, "I have given you an example to follow. Do as I have done to you" (John 13.15). Service in a Christian framework is not optional; it is central to life's purpose. In an educational setting, Boyer speaks to the balance between being autonomous individuals while also being accountable to the community. He stresses that undergraduates "urgently need to see the relationship between what they learn and how they live" (218). Specifically Boyer urges students—and faculty—to use their knowledge for the good of the larger community, to engage in service that strengthens the fabric of the community. This obligation to serve and to use one's gifts to better society reminds me of the Bible's exhortation that "to whom much is given, much is expected" (Luke 12.48). Receiving a college education was, for me, a high privilege and working in an academic community is, in my view, an honorable way to make a living and a life. Increasingly, however, I have become aware that with privilege comes responsibility. My position requires that I give something back, that I use my gifts for the benefit of others. Once again I am reminded of the words I've heard Betty Siegel say countless times: "Service is the rent you pay on the time and space you spend on earth."

In addition to the importance of my spirituality and its influence on the way I view relationships, community, and service, a second value that runs throughout all that I do is a genuine and lifelong love of teaching and learning. From my earliest days when I arranged my dolls in a make-believe classroom, I have known that I wanted to be a teacher. Indeed, it was for me a "calling" rather than simply a career choice. What I've come to see, however, is that there are multiple "classrooms," many without walls, and different venues that lie outside the traditional classroom setting. After completing my PhD in English literature and being tenured in the English Department at KSU, I felt that my future was indeed set: I would live out my days teaching English as I had always planned I would do. At Dr. Siegel's urging I made a move into administration. I clearly recall saying to her, "I very much appreciate your offer but I am a teacher; I could never be an administrator." But I also vividly remember her response: "Nancy, there are many ways to be a teacher that are not confined to the classroom." After almost 20 years in administration, I have come to see that she was indeed correct. I would add that my teaching has not been limited to the KSU campus. In my roles as an adult Sunday school teacher, book club facilitator, presenter and speaker at professional conferences, and as a consultant in higher education I continually draw upon my teaching abilities. In addition, I am very aware that even in my interactions with my grandchildren I am also privileged to be teaching. What a joy to introduce them to the poems that I read to their parents before them or to watch their eyes widen as the mystery of reading unfolds or some bit of knowledge about the world around them clicks into place.

At the same time that I am teaching, however, I am also learning. Quite often my role as the "teacher" for our students and for the directors in my division morphs into that of a "learner" because I truly learn from those I'm charged with teaching and directing. What I experience on a daily basis is the knowledge that indeed I do not have all the answers, and I am quite often stunned by the keen insights and solutions presented by those I'm privileged to work alongside. Once again I am reminded of an observation Dr. Siegel is fond of making. As I have heard her say many times: "On your own you may have a few good ideas, but in working with others those ideas multiply many times over." With every passing year in administration I have become more convinced of the power of thinking and communicating with others. One person's idea sparks another and the process of "group thinking" leads to far more ideas than I could ever have had in isolation. I remember fondly the experience of developing a mission statement for our new Division of Student Success and Enrollment Services soon after I became vice president. The directors and I met in a retreat at the Jolley Lodge, a meeting facility at KSU, and the process of creating a mission for our new division was an excellent illustration of the value of a team approach. Years later, we followed the same group format in revamping our mission statement in response to growth and change. Certainly King Solomon was correct in observing that "Iron sharpens iron, so one man sharpens another" (Proverbs 27.17).

Perhaps what is most exciting to me is the realization that opportunities for teaching and for learning never end. As the members of my book club and I have so often remarked, there will always be new books to read, cultures to explore, and things to understand. As I age, I become more and more convinced that the core value of learning will forever be an important part of my life. I have also come to terms with how little I truly know. Indeed, I have traveled a far distance from the somewhat cocky young undergraduate who felt that my 4.0 GPA meant I had mastered a great deal of knowledge to a belief that I have only begun to scratch the surface of all there is to know. Each day presents new opportunities to stretch my thinking and to expand my understanding of the world around me.

I have become increasingly concerned, however, that the teaching and learning that I consider to be the centerpiece of the academy is in danger of falling behind a new emphasis on retaining and graduating students. Instead of focusing on "learners," we appear to be more and more concerned with "graduates." Without question graduation should be the goal of college students; however, my sincere hope is that in the rush to exit our colleges and universities students not lose sight of the importance of what they are learning and the relevance that knowledge will have to their future lives. Chittister has an excellent commentary on the Rule of St. Benedict:

> Benedict teaches that life is a learning process. Western culture and its emphasis on academic degrees, however, has almost smothered this truth. We have made the words "graduation" and "education" almost synonymous. We measure achievement in academic credits. We discount experience, depth, and failure . . . all of that kind of achievement is nothing but a spiritual wasteland if along the way we have not attached ourselves to the discovery of truth, the cultivation of beauty, and the recognition of the real learnings of life. (qtd. in Vaill 191)

Benedict has expressed eloquently my feelings about teaching and learning, and I am reminded of what I have heard Dr. Siegel say so often: "College is not a collection of courses or a ticket to a trade." She believes passionately—as do I—that education does far more than simply prepare us to make a living; rather, it enables us to make a more meaningful life.

Yet another insight I have come to understand about teaching and learning relates to the idea of exactly who serves as the "teacher." On the surface, all of us in higher education would agree that teaching is an act performed by faculty inside the classroom. Certainly, that is for the most part true. However, I have increasingly become aware of the teaching that goes on by faculty outside the walls of the classroom and by non-faculty as well. I very much like Parker Palmer's observation in an Afterword for *Creating Campus Community* that "the notion that 'we are all teachers' is not romanticism" (181). He goes on to explain that students learn not only from classroom lectures, readings and discussions, but from what researchers call "the hidden curriculum," which Palmer defines as "the way individual and collective life is lived on a campus—from the way the people employed there do their work, conduct their relationships, make their choices, and otherwise reveal their true values, which may be quite at odds with the values espoused in the classroom" (18l). For this reason I have become keenly aware that my life and example "teach" and that there must be a very real alignment between the values I claim to hold and the way I conduct myself on campus and beyond. For example, if I claim to honor lifelong learning, but I never demonstrate any involvement in learning activities, there is an obvious disconnect between my words and my actions.

In addition to my spiritual foundation and a passion for teaching and learning, a third value that is woven throughout all of my roles is an intense interest and fascination with people. My Myers-Briggs type indicates that I am a strong extrovert. I am by nature inclined to talk to strangers in stores and to seatmates on airplanes. In fact, nothing is more fascinating to me than interaction with my fellow human beings. This is a characteristic that has been most helpful to me in both my personal and professional lives because of the importance of relationships. In order to establish relationships and to understand others it is critical to know something about their stories—and all people regardless of whom they are or where they come from have a story to tell. While the earlier part of my life was spent primarily with those who were very much like me, what has been one of the greatest rewards of a life spent in higher education is the opportunity to get outside my comfort zone and to meet and interact with those who are fundamentally different from me in race, ethnicity, socioeconomic background, faith, and sexual orientation. This incredible range of people has made my life far richer and more interesting than it would have been had my interactions been confined to those who are like me.

As a member of a university community I have participated in numerous workshops on diversity, and I have attended countless lectures and presentations on this topic. What has made the most lasting impact on me, however, has been the opportunity to get to know diverse students, staff, and faculty and to hear their stories and unique perspectives. In addition, the chance to travel internationally has helped to expand my boundaries far beyond my south Georgia roots and has given me a greater understanding of different cultures and approaches to life. This valuing of diverse cultures and viewpoints is at the very core of higher education. Indeed, a university cannot long survive in an atmosphere of restricting a free exchange of diverse ideas. At the heart of what we value in society is a belief that all people deserve to be treated fairly. In the process of interacting with those who differ from me in race, culture, religion, or sexual orientation, I have developed a far greater appreciation for the need for equity, regardless of differences, that I might not have learned as readily outside the academy.

Another of my mentors and role models, Dr. Virginia N. Gordon, played a major role in my academic life. Dr. Gordon, who is now retired from The Ohio State University, is perhaps the foremost expert in the country on academic advising and the contributions it makes to student development. One of the proudest moments in my professional life has to be when I received the Virginia N. Gordon Award for Excellence in Academic Advising presented by the National Academic Advising Association. My pride stemmed from having my name associated with a woman whom I respect and admire so profoundly. In a reader for college students, *Foundations*, edited by Dr. Gordon and Thomas L. Minnick, diversity is closely linked to dialogue. The editors admit that defining dialogue is not easy; but they relate it to the way the nineteenth-century Catholic philosopher John Henry, Cardinal Newman, and the early twentieth-century Jewish teacher Martin Buber understood dialogue: "one person speaking to another, heart to heart, and listening . . . . the result of dialogue is often to understand oneself better through understanding someone else . . . . Dialogue is the means by which we discover and evaluate truth, and diversity is the starting point for dialogue" (210-11).

One of the greatest advantages of being part of a university is the opportunity to engage in dialogue not only with colleagues and students, but with a wide range of distinguished lecturers and guests to our campus. I am amazed by what I've learned from the truly outstanding and diverse group of individuals who have visited our campus as part of the Chautauqua lecture series, a program sponsored by the Kennesaw Activities Board composed of KSU students. Poet Maya Angelou, educator Jamie Escalante, Native-American leader N. Scott Momaday, astronaut Mae Jemison, journalists Helen Thomas and Yaron Svoray, former United States Surgeon General Dr. Jocelyn Elders, filmmaker and adventurer David Breshears, actor James Earl Jones—these are but a few of the accomplished individuals in the Chautauqua lecture series whom I have been honored to meet. Hearing these individuals speak and, in most cases, having the pleasure of sharing dinner and dialogue with them has provided extremely stimulating and thought-provoking experiences for me.

A final common thread that is woven throughout my life is my attitude toward success and leadership. My title at KSU, Vice President for Student Success and Enrollment Services, even includes the word "success," and the designation "vice president" implies that I am a leader. But my attitude towards both success and leadership has changed quite a bit over the years. Clearly, success is far more than material gains, although I have accomplished more in that area than I would have dreamed starting out as a part-time English instructor at Kennesaw Junior College. There is a sharp contrast between making money and making a difference, between being successful and being valuable. At this point in my life, success is measured far more by the following three standards. My first measurement of success is a sense of fulfillment—a feeling that what I am doing in all areas of life "matters" and has a positive impact on others. I remember quite vividly a visit from a student many years ago. This student, whom I had come to know quite well, stopped by my office to share some good news with me. Her face glowed as she told me that she had been named to the President's List spring semester as a result of her 4.0 GPA. What pleased me most as I listened to the pride in her voice was the memory of my first encounter with her, a single mother coming to college for the very first time. We met during advisement at new student orientation. I remembered clearly her anxiety and fear. In fact, I recalled her saying to me with tears in her eyes, "I just don't think I can do this; I'm really scared!" We became better acquainted because she was a student in one of my classes, and I was delighted to see her gradually let go of her fears as she became increasingly confident of her abilities. With every passing term she stretched a bit more and surprised herself with her new knowledge and accomplishments. What a joy to have a job where I am allowed to see firsthand students discover their capacity to succeed. It is like having a front row seat to watch miracles unfold.

A second measure of success for me today is the ability to possess what the Bible calls "the fruits of the spirit—love, joy, peace, goodness, kindness, faithfulness, gentleness, patience and self-control" (Galatians 5.22). Developing these attributes is far more important to my definition of success than amassing wealth or adding to my résumé. Certainly God intends for us to mature in our faith. In his letters to the churches at Corinth and at Ephesus, the apostle Paul contrasts the mature Christian with the immature. In 1 Corinthians 3.1-4, Paul writes: "I've been talking to you like babies in the Christian life, who are not following the Lord, but your own desires; I cannot talk to you as I would mature Christians who are filled with the spirit." Being filled with the Spirit to the point that we continually abide in Christ is evidence of Christian maturity. When that happens, we no longer segment our lives and ration out only moments or hours to fellowship with our Lord. Rather, we continually practice the presence of God. I have always loved the famous observation from Brother Lawrence, a lay brother among the seventeenth-century Carmelites, that even in the noise and clutter of his kitchen he feels God's presence as surely as if he were upon his knees in prayer.

With this kind of spiritual maturity comes the ultimate in balance—aligning one's spirit with all the physical, emotional, and mental dimensions of life. At this stage in my life, I have realized that the balance that grows out of spiritual maturity gives me a quiet confidence that causes my faith to be unmoved regardless of the changing circumstances of life. As a maturing Christian, I believe I am less vulnerable to the latest fad doctrines or self-help gurus that fill our airwaves and bookshelves than I would be without my faith. As Paul says in his letter to the Ephesians regarding spiritual maturity:

> Then we will no longer be like children, forever changing our minds about what we believe because someone has told us something different, or has cleverly lied to us and made the lie sound like the truth. Instead, we will lovingly follow the truth at all times—speaking truly, dealing truly, living truly— and so become more and more in every way like Christ who is the head of his body, the church. Under his direction the whole body is fitted together perfectly, and each part in its own special way helps the other parts, so that the whole body is healthy and growing and full of love. (Ephesians 4.14-16)

Here Paul has given us a beautiful image of the spiritually mature church, characterized by unity in diversity and filled with love and a commitment to truth. In order to fulfill God's plan for this loving, mature church, it is necessary for the individual members to grow spiritually. For me, this spiritual growth is a key measurement of my success.

A third way I have come to measure success is by the opportunities I have to expand my view of the world and experience new things. Being able to travel internationally has broadened my perspective far beyond what I could ever have imagined. As I reflect over my travels, many vivid images float through my mind—climbing the Great Wall in China, snorkeling at the Great Barrier Reef in Australia, kneeling before the birthplace of Christ at the Church of the Nativity, standing in Red Square in Moscow, gazing in awe at the waterfalls of Milford Sound in New Zealand and the spectacular beauty of the Dingle Peninsula in Ireland, catching my first glimpse of the wonders of Petra in Jordan. These memories constitute success because of the amazing array of experiences they represent. Without leaving home I can also expand my horizons—books; films; professional conferences; speakers at the university, church, and community groups have enlarged my world view, and that for me translates into success.

As my definition of success has shifted over the years, so, too, has my understanding of leadership. There was a time years ago when I believed that the leader was the one "in charge" or the person who was responsible. Usually, I thought, one could tell from a person's title or position whether or not he or she was indeed the leader in an organization. I now see, however, that leadership is not defined by titles nor is it static. This change in my view of leadership has come about as a result of many experiences and from the many different roles that I play in my life. For example, the changing relationships within my family demonstrate that leadership is dynamic, not static. I have watched my three children mature into bright, accomplished individuals who now frequently take the lead. I remember well the first Thanksgiving at my daughter's house and the moment I realized that Lisa, an amazingly competent young woman, had moved into the role I had once played as the "leader" in this holiday tradition. I also think of the pride I have felt when I hear someone refer to "Dr. King" and I realize that the reference is to my oldest son, David, who has followed my footsteps into higher education. Watching my "baby" Allen excel in his career and develop into an exemplary father has been another source of enormous satisfaction for me. There can be no doubt but that my crowning achievement in leadership resulted from the gift of parenting these three remarkable individuals and watching them mature into the leaders they have each become in their own right.

In my professional role as Vice President for Student Success and Enrollment Services (SSES) at Kennesaw State, I have grown to value highly the leadership of inclusion. True, I am ultimately responsible and accountable for the workings of our division, but one of the rewards of my job is working as a part of a team made up of an invaluable assistant and the SSES directors. I am very aware of the roles shifting back and forth between the leader and the followers depending on the circumstances. There are times, for example, when one of the directors will assume the lead and the others of us will follow. Since my spirituality has permeated all areas of my life, I have also come to believe that true leadership is directly related to service. In the words of Christ: "Whoever wants to be a leader among you must be your servant . . . for even I, the Son of Man, came here not to be served, but to serve" (Matthew 20.26). "But among you the one who serves you best will be your leader" (Luke 22.25). There can be no mistaking the strong correlation between leadership and service in a Christian construct. Likewise, there can be no question but that leadership must be ethical, another lesson I have learned from working with Betty Siegel over the past 25 years.

One of the greatest rewards at this stage of my career has been facilitating the leadership skills of younger professionals who are poised to step into the roles held by my generation. Not only do I learn daily from my interaction with these talented young leaders, but I find a great deal of satisfaction in mentoring them and assisting their career development. In addition, it is extremely rewarding to see the achievements of students I have worked with over the years. I remember with great fondness the many students who have left Kennesaw State to pursue graduate work and those who have excelled in their chosen professions. Last week, I visited with a young man, a former outstanding student leader at KSU, who is now a graduate of Harvard Law School and associated with one of Atlanta's premier law firms, and I realized once again how very blessed I am to play a small part in students' lives and to witness their becoming the embodiment of "student success."

As I think back over my journey, I am struck by the important roles mentors have played in my life. There have been many individuals who have shaped me throughout the years, but there is no question but that my life reflects the enormous influence of Dr. Betty Siegel. Speaking of spiritual guides, Nouwen refers to those people in our lives "who speak the language of our heart and give us courage" (19). These people, Nouwen says, "are our guides. Not to be imitated but to help us live our lives just as authentically as they live theirs. When we have found such guides we have good reason to be grateful and even better reason to listen attentively to what they have to say" (19). In my professional life, Dr. Betty Siegel has, without question, been that guide for me. Her example and her inspiring philosophy of how to live one's life have been profound influences in helping me achieve balance, and for that I am most grateful. She has truly modeled the way for me as I have grown to understand more clearly the pivotal role core values play in all areas of my life.

In all honesty, I simply cannot imagine Kennesaw State without Dr. Betty L. Siegel at the helm as its president. What she has done for me in terms of inspiration and motivation she has done for countless others. Her unflappable optimism; her gracious, inviting manner; her deep appreciation for the power of relationships; her passion for education; and her insistence on ethics and character—all have been hallmarks of Dr. Siegel's leadership style. Even though she is stepping down as president of our university, of one thing I am absolutely certain: Betty Siegel will continue to make significant contributions to this campus and far beyond because she is the quintessential "lifelong learner," and her capacity for growth and achievement seem limitless. Like so many others, I owe her an enormous debt of gratitude because her influence on my life over the past 25 years helped shape the person I am today. I am better because our paths have been woven so closely over a quarter of a century.

When I consider the many initiatives I have been privileged to work alongside Dr. Siegel to accomplish, I am aware of how profoundly I have been influenced by what she values most in education. The First-Year Experience and the Senior-Year Experience Programs reflect her keen awareness of the importance of transitions in students' lives; her emphasis on community-building activities and service learning underscores her belief in the value of relationships and the importance of giving something back; and the Institute for Leadership, Ethics, and Character (ILEC) resulted from her vision and emphasis on the importance of ethical leadership.

It is quite simply impossible to envision what my professional life would have been without her wise counsel and guidance. In the same way that our university themes each year have bourne the stamp of Dr. Siegel's vision and values, my life also reflects her influence. One of these annual themes illustrates a core value in Dr. Siegel's life: "From Success to Significance." Obviously, she has been most successful as a leader in higher education far beyond the Kennesaw campus, but most important, she has engaged in significant work. I am confident that she has made a profound impact on the lives of many in the same way that she has mine. I am equally confident that I will continue to look to her example as she models the way towards wintering into wisdom.

Works Cited

Boyer, Ernest L. *College: The Undergraduate Experience in America.* New York: Harper and Row, 1987.

Gordon, Virginia M., and Thomas L. Minnick. *Foundations: A Reader for New College Students.* Belmont: Wadsworth, 1996.

McMillen, Kim. "The Workplace as Spiritual Haven." *When the Canary Stops Singing: Women's Perspectives on Transforming Business.* Ed. Pat Barrentine. San Francisco: Barret-Koehler, 1993. 105-118.

Nouwen, Henri J. M. *The Only Necessary Thing.* Ed. Wendy Wilson Greer. New York: Crossroads, 1999.

Palmer, Parker. Afterword. *Creating Campus Community: In Search of Ernest Boyer's Legacy.* Ed. William M. McDonald. San Francisco: Jossey Bass, 2002. ix-xvi.

Vaill, Peter B. *Learning as a Way of Being: Strategies for Survival in a World of Permanent White Water.* San Francisco: Jossey Bass, 1996.

The Secrets of Life: Planning, Collaboration, Improvisation

Joseph D. Meeks

When I was a small boy growing up in South Carolina, we didn't have video games or television to keep us entertained. Instead, we spent much of our time "visiting" with family. In those days, my favorite place in the world was my Aunt Ophelia's house. She had very little money, but she had wisdom and loving beyond measure.

After supper, she would pour coffee into delicate cups and saucers for everyone, including the children. When we had nothing left but the grounds, she would take each cup and gently swirl the remains. Then, she would gaze intently into the grounds and "read" our futures—always filled with success and happiness. "I see an ocean," she would say. "I think you are going to go to Europe." "I can see you on the concert stage," she told me once, and my mind filled with visions of a future that could be.

After learning all the secrets of the future, she would walk over to a simple box in the corner that she had decorated with cloth from a flour sack. From this little treasure chest, she ceremoniously withdrew a bag of chocolate drops, and each of us delighted over our single, delicious taste of heaven.

But the real highlight of the evening was the jigsaw puzzle. Every house in my family always had a jigsaw puzzle in progress. We were always "working" a puzzle. Piece by piece, together we would assemble a glorious painting or photo. At Aunt Ophelia's house, we all gathered around the puzzle. Each new discovery was a celebration.

We congratulated the member of the family who found new insight, new vision—the person who, in that moment, brought the picture more clearly into view.

I like to think Aunt Ophelia knew the secret of life for which we are always seeking. She was a humble woman of humble circumstance, but she had an inner wisdom and strength that still speak to me today.

Now that my hair is a much different color than it used to be, I think I can comprehend and articulate some of the wisdom of Aunt Ophelia. The secret of life is the same as the secret to success, and it is certainly the secret of the arts.

The secret is this: planning, collaboration, and improvisation.

In order to succeed, you must first carefully lay a foundation, outline your goals, know where you are going, and have at least a passing idea of how you are going to get there.

And although we all know all of the pitfalls and jokes about committees, we must never underrate the value of collaboration. As I have heard Dr. Betty Siegel, President Emerita of Kennesaw State University, say, "we are altogether better because we are all together." We need input and advice and vision from others to put the puzzle together. Imagine an orchestra without the strings. Or a play written by the greatest playwright directed by the brightest young director with no actors on the stage. Neither the play nor the concert can ever be whole without everyone in place. Even the solo performer and the visual artist working alone in the studio rely on collaboration from the past (the instructor who gave insight or the influence who inspired) as well as collaboration in the future (the viewer who will see the work, the reviewer who will critique it) to provide guidance and direction in the moment of creativity.

Finally, you must be able to improvise. We all have experienced a project, a program, a vacation or a dinner party thrown into chaos when the unexpected occurs. How well we are able to work from memory when the PowerPoint presentation doesn't work, find another way to navigate Venice when the gondoliers go on strike, or hurriedly prepare a new dessert when the torch gets too close to the crème brûlée, is a true sign of our ability to survive, thrive, and succeed.

Improvisation

Several years ago, we invited a talented, young Brazilian pianist named José Feghali to perform at Kennesaw State. He had played at the university before, so we already knew he was a powerful and flexible performer, but we had no idea how terrific he really could be. A couple of weeks before Mr. Feghali's concert, we discovered that our theater had developed a small leak in the roof over the stage. We formulated a plan to address the problem temporarily and then repair it between academic sessions. It was a minor problem really, an occasional nuisance for the people who worked on the stage every day.

Then, just before Mr. Feghali's performance, it began to rain. And it rained. And it rained. By the time of the concert, we were in the middle of a torrential thunderstorm. Tornado sirens were being sounded in our area, but to our complete surprise and delight, the audience came.

Then, the problems started; the little leak in the back corner grew and spread. Trickles of water dripped in several locations on the stage, but it still did not seem very serious. We postponed the concert momentarily as the stage crew worked with mops and towels to dry the floor.

Then, Mr. Feghali took the stage. The audience enthusiastically received his first few pieces, but I watched in horror as puddles began forming in several locations on stage and one steady, malicious drop after another began to hit the piano we had rented from the Steinway Piano Gallery. I looked around the theater, hoping the 18 members of the Atlanta Steinway Society who were attending their very first KSU concert hadn't noticed.

Between pieces, Mr. Feghali patiently waited in the wings while the crew shifted the piano to a drier position. He made not one word of complaint, although many pianists would be infuriated about a piano being moved after it had been finely tuned.

With a gracious smile he returned to the stage and completed the first half of the concert. During intermission, I became increasingly anxious. Between responding to Dr. Siegel's earnest inquiries about what we were going to do, chatting pleasantly with our guests, and urgently insisting to my staff that something must be done, I briefly considered running out into the thunderstorm.

After intermission, we gathered back into the theater, the lights dimmed; we could hear the rain outside and see it on the stage. Mr. Feghali emerged on to the stage with a spring in his step and an umbrella over his head! He waltzed across the stage as the audience laughed, and everyone joyfully joined in as he played "Happy Birthday" in honor of Dr. Siegel. We all left that concert a little less serious and, perhaps, a little richer than when we arrived.

We will still continue to encounter moments that call for improvisation on a regular, sometimes daily, basis. We are fortunate, however, to have a wonderful team of faculty, staff, and students in the College of the Arts, whose creativity, positive spirit, and ability to collaborate help us through those moments of stress and opportunity.

Collaboration

Collaboration, of course, extends well beyond moments of crisis. The nature of our business is collaboration. We actively seek ways to join with others to set new goals and to attain them. In 2002, one of our faculty members, Dr. Laurence Sherr, created an opportunity for collaboration that led to one of the most powerful and moving moments in my life.

Dr. Sherr, a composer-in-residence at Kennesaw State, had found tremendous success composing instrumental music for small ensembles, orchestras, and solo musicians. For his first choral composition, he used poetry written by Holocaust survivor Nelly Sachs to create a work called "Fugitive Footsteps," which he dedicated to his mother, who is also a Holocaust survivor. Realizing that his new composition could be used for various Holocaust remembrance events, Dr. Sherr approached Cantor Deborah Binardot at The Temple on Peachtree Street in Atlanta. Together, they decided to stage a concert featuring "Fugitive Footsteps" and other works by Jewish composers. Cantor Binardot secured sponsorship from Rabbi Alvin Sugarman, and Dr. Sherr asked for the College of the Arts to co-sponsor the event. I immediately said yes and agreed to speak during the program.

Meanwhile, Dr. Sherr began seeking musicians to perform "Fugitive Footsteps" and the other music. In the end, he invited one of the best choral directors he knew, Kennesaw State's own Dr. Leslie Blackwell, to prepare her elite ensemble, the KSU Chamber Singers, to take up the challenge. The student singers, Dr. Blackwell, and Dr. Sherr worked with a guest baritone, Cantor Daniel Gale from a synagogue in Michigan, to bring the new work to life. Then, the KSU Women's Ensemble and two more musicians, pianist David Watkins, KSU Professor of Music, and cellist Nan Maddox, signed on to perform that evening, and a program of profoundly moving music was selected.

On the evening of the performance, even though a thunderstorm was again raging, Holocaust survivors, members of the Jewish community, campus friends, and music lovers gathered at The Temple in Atlanta. As the Women's Ensemble sang "I Never Saw Another Butterfly," with poetry written by children at the Terezin Concentration Camp, in what is now the Czech Republic, I began to feel a certain fellowship embracing the audience—together we mourned and together we celebrated the triumph of the human spirit.

That evening, my prepared remarks addressed the topic that music and the arts have the power to bring communities together, and I reminded the audience that we are among the last people who will ever know a Holocaust survivor. I believed every word I said, but even I did not understand the full meaning of my words.

Slowly, a realization began to creep into my mind. I listened, amazed, as the KSU Chamber Singers, a group of young men and women from diverse backgrounds, sang the haunting melodies of Dr. Sherr's new work, "Fugitive Footsteps." For these young people, Hitler is a historical figure as remote as Attila the Hun; but from working with this music, in preparing to perform it, they had been transformed. They were able to convey the suffering and mourning of Nelly Sachs' poem and Dr. Sherr's score.

Around me, people periodically dabbed handkerchiefs at their eyes. Jews and gentiles together felt the power of the human spirit. That night, through collaboration and through the arts, we built a bridge between people. By the time Dr. Sherr presented a signed score to his mother everyone in the Temple had a different understanding of the human cost of the Holocaust and the triumph of the individuals who survived.

But I still didn't get the full message until an older woman, another Holocaust survivor, told me that this very special concert brought her a sense of healing that she had never experienced before. She told me she never would have guessed that her healing would come from a little town called Kennesaw, Georgia.

Finally, I understood entirely.

The power of collaboration is larger than the two people or three people who come together. Our strength and understanding grow exponentially when we come to the table together.

Planning

Of course, a lot of planning went into that collaboration at The Temple that evening. For months, we prepared for it. We rehearsed and created programs, consulted light designers and sound recorders, set up equipment, designed ads, and sent information to synagogues throughout the area.

Planning is essential to success. If you don't know where you are going when you get in your car to drive, you are never going to get there.

For some projects, planning may take a couple of days or a month or two. Sometimes, planning takes years, but if the goal is worthy, you should pour your resources into it until you accomplish it.

When the College of the Arts was created and I was invited to be its first dean in 1998, we knew we were on the verge of great things. We had just emerged from a tremendous year of celebration. The entire university had come together to celebrate "The Year of the Arts." American opera legend Beverly Sills spoke at our annual university convocation. Faculty across campus, regardless of discipline, incorporated aspects of the arts into their curricula. Public programming expanded and the community attended in record numbers. Enrollment increased and the media really began to pay attention to what we were doing in the arts. Everyone was excited and energized. We were all ready to take the next big step.

That summer, the Departments of Music, Theater, and Visual Arts were separated from the College of Arts, Humanities, and Social Sciences to form the new College of the Arts. The new academic structure allowed the university to better focus and prioritize its goals for the arts. My faculty and I immediately set to work to move to the next level.

At that time, only the Department of Music had received national accreditation. The accreditation process is exhaustive and exhausting. Institutions are subjected to extremely thorough reviews of academic requirements, faculty qualifications, facilities, public programming, funding, marketing, and many other aspects of their operations. After accreditation is accomplished, institutions must continue to adhere to the high standards set by the agency or risk losing accreditation.

Music had met and was maintaining those standards. We knew theater and visual arts were also performing at a very high level, but they had not been evaluated to see if they met the criteria for accreditation. First, the Department of Theatre applied for recognition from the National Association of Schools of Theater (NAST). The faculty completed a yearlong self-study of its programs, faculty, admissions standards, and all of the other required elements. Then, NAST external reviewers visited campus, examined documents, visited classes, interviewed faculty and students, and checked every item in the self-study report. A few months later, we received the happy news that accreditation had been awarded.

But we didn't rest long on our laurels. The Department of Visual Arts already had launched its application for accreditation by the National Association of Schools of Art and Design (NASAD). The faculty conducted research, prepared reports, and met weekly to complete the self-study report as the music faculty and theater faculty had done before. With the self-study finally completed, a NASAD visitation team conducted a very thorough review. When the evaluation team left, they delivered a positive report, but we still had to wait months for the final affirmative decision. With that third piece of the puzzle in place, Kennesaw State University became only the fourth school in Georgia to achieve full accreditation for all of its arts programs.

That didn't happen overnight. It didn't happen without planning. It didn't happen without improvisation. And it didn't happen without collaboration.

The real secret of life is that success is a process, not a destination—another lesson learned from Aunt Ophelia so many years ago.

Portrait of a Cheerful Leader

William Watson Purkey

Gerald Ford, in his eulogy for Hugh Sidney, quoted what his friend had written, "Joy in one's heart and some laughter on one's lips is a sign that the person deep down has a pretty good grasp on life" (A25). This certainly sounds like a portrait of the most cheerful leader I have ever known, Betty Faye Siegel, coal miner's daughter.

The Need for Cheerful Leadership

I doubt that there has ever been a greater need for cheerful leaders. As this is written, the world finds itself in "another fine mess," as the portly Mr. Oliver Hardy of Laurel and Hardy fame would say. Television, newspapers, radio, newsmagazines, the Internet, and countless other information outlets remind us constantly of worldwide warming, deadly hurricanes, floods, tsunamis, bird flu pandemics, and other natural catastrophes. This grim news is coupled with the frustration of an apparently endless war, terrorist plots, the deepening national debt, disappointment and anger over rising fuel prices, and bribed politicians. A friend and colleague, Eddie Collins, summed it all up, "We are in a mean-spirited time."

To paraphrase a song, "What the world needs now, is cheerfulness, sweet cheerfulness." Betty Siegel is a major source of sweet cheerfulness. Her affirmation of cheerfulness is a declaration of the human spirit and an inspiration to everyone who knows her.

Betty Siegel as a Model of Cheerful Leadership

I have had the pleasure of working closely with Betty for over four decades. Our two families have "birthed babies and buried kin." Looking back, I can truly say that she has one of the most cheerful hearts I have ever encountered. I have been with her when terrible weather stranded us in small airports, when family health problems loomed large, when audiences were as cold as ice, and when very difficult and painful executive decisions had to be made. She handles challenging situations with intelligence, empathy, concern, and above all, cheerfulness. A good description of Betty would be "the unsinkable Molly Brown."

A true story illustrates Betty's cheerful nature in the face of calamity. Back when the earth was cooling and dinosaurs ruled, Betty and I were young hot-shot assistant professors at the University of Florida. Both of us were highly successful teachers and had already won university awards for excellence in teaching. We thought we were invincible.

When the superintendent of a large Florida school system called and offered to pay us to team-teach an evening extension course for some "struggling" teachers, we leaped at the opportunity. The class was named "Becoming an Inviting Teacher." Meetings were scheduled for one night a week for eight weeks.

What we were not told, and found out many weeks later, was that the class consisted of 35 tenure-track, burned-out educators whose relations with others were somewhere between terrible and horrible. The class was the superintendent's final effort to turn these teachers around and help them to be more inviting to themselves and to parents, students, and colleagues, personally and professionally. The 35 teachers did not want to take our class. They had the choice of taking the class or of being fired.

We began the first class meeting with great self-confidence and exaggerated pride. (The ancient Greeks called it "hubris.") Betty started the first class off with some of her wonderful stories and cheerful attitude. Nothing happened. It was like teaching to terra-cotta soldiers buried in a Chinese emperor's tomb.

Then it was my turn. I pushed Betty aside, introduced myself, made some very funny (to me) comments, and started a lesson. Again, there was absolutely no response, other than cold stares. The terra-cotta teachers were giving us nothing.

After three hours of complete failure, we ended the class and headed home to Gainesville. During our drive back we reassured each other that our opening failure was an aberration. We were award-winning teachers. Top guns! How could we lose?

In preparation for the second class, Betty and I developed a fail-proof lesson plan, guaranteed to succeed. Then we headed back to our second class meeting, heavily armed with audio-visuals, extensive notes, and exercises. Again, we bombed.

In the following five weeks we tried every trick in the teacher's notebook. Nothing worked. The terra-cotta teachers were wearing us down. Betty and I began to lose our confidence. We would stop at a Dairy Queen on the way back from our latest debacle and buy milkshakes. We would look at each other mournfully and suck on our straws. It was clear that we were being punished by Nemesis, the Greek goddess of fate and punisher of extravagant pride.

After the seventh class meeting of our scheduled eight weeks in hell, we had one class left. We were committed to face the terra-cotta teachers one last time. We could not bear to do it. We hired an even younger top-gun professor, Alan Dobbs, to travel with us and work with the teachers. Betty and I would sit in the back of the classroom and watch. Better his blood than ours.

To our astonishment, Alan Dobbs was a smash hit! The terra-cotta teachers laughed, interacted, and seemed to love him as much as they disliked us. Betty and I never figured out the dynamics of how he did it.

The point of the terra-cotta teacher story is that throughout this very challenging experience, Betty always maintained her sense of humor and her cheerful approach to challenges. When I would lose hope, she would say something like this, "Come on, Purkey, pull up your socks. We'll get them next week." We never did "get them," but I'll always remember Betty's cheerful manner in facing the terra-cotta teachers. She rises above difficulties like a kite rising high against the wind . . . .

The Value of Cheerfulness

In my book, *Teaching Class Clowns (And What They Can Teach Us)*, I explored the value of cheerfulness. I explained that cheerfulness is a quality of good spirit, joy, optimism, and gladness that warms the hearts of most people.

Cheerfulness differs from happiness, which is a consistent feeling of well-being and contentment. Cheerful leaders may not be happy, but they are of good spirit. Examples of cheerful leaders would be Franklin Roosevelt, Ronald Reagan, Hubert Humphrey, Bob Dole, and Bill Clinton. They seem to follow Shakespeare's advice, "Lay aside life-harming heaviness and entertain a cheerful disposition" (*Richard II* 2.1.3-4).

President Ronald Reagan exhibited the wonderful qualities of a cheerful leader under extreme stress. Immediately after he had been wounded in an assassination attempt, his first comment to his wife Nancy was, "Honey, I forgot to duck" (244). (He was repeating what Jack Dempsey commented after losing his heavyweight title to Gene Tunney in 1926.) Later that day, as a surgeon was about to operate on him, Reagan said, "I hope you're a Republican" (245). Reagan's cheerful spirit, even in the face of deadly danger, placed him among the most likeable and admired of presidents. Even political adversaries admired his cheerful spirit.

The words "cheer" and "cheerful" have a rich history. In the *King James Bible* the terms appear often. However, in later translations (i.e. *The Complete Bible: An American Translation*), "cheer" and "cheerful" have been changed to "courage" and "courageous." It is interesting to note that "*cor,*" the Latin word for "heart," is the basis for the word "courage." Both cheer and courage are invitations to take heart and to be of good spirit. Both terms describe the up-beat approach to life exhibited by cheerful leaders.

President Franklin D. Roosevelt demonstrated remarkable cheerfulness when he responded to charges that he had sent a destroyer to transport his dog back home. In his regular "fireside chats" radio address, Roosevelt replied to critics:

> These Republican leaders have not been content with attacks on me, or on my wife, or on my sons. No, not content with that, they now include my little dog Fala. Well, of course I don't resent attacks, and my family doesn't resent attacks, but Fala does resent them. (qtd. in Goodwin 548)

Roosevelt's humorous comment took the wind out of hostile critics. He was truly a cheerful leader.

Six Signature Tendencies of Cheerful Leaders

Martin Seligman, in his book *Authentic Happiness* identifies "signature strengths." These strengths are characteristics of those who experience authentic happiness. Using Seligman's framework of signature strengths, I have identified six signature strengths that cheerful leaders value and seek to practice every day. These six strengths are presented in the form of axioms:

1. Know thyself, but don't take thyself too seriously
2. Savor every moment of your life
3. Find humor in frustrations
4. Fight fair
5. Challenge authority
6. Believe that any attempt is a victory.

Each of these signature strengths of cheerful leaders will be considered in turn.

Know Thyself, but Don't Take Thyself too Seriously. According to Bertrand Russell, one of the warning signs of an approaching heart attack, stroke, or nervous breakdown is the belief that one's work is terribly important. A number of scientific studies (see Seligman) indicate that a light-hearted approach to life, as measured by the Multidimensional Sense of Humor Scale (MSHS) relates positively to a number of factors associated with psychological health. Negative scores on the MSHS are associated with psychological stress and depression.

A delightful example of cheerfulness was provided by Stanley Laurel, of Laurel and Hardy fame. Stan was lying in his hospital room during his final days. A nurse entered his room to administer emergency assistance. Stan looked up and said, "You know what? I'd a lot rather be skiing." The nurse responded, "Do you ski, Mr. Laurel?" He said, "No, but I'd a lot rather be skiing than doing this" (McCabe 37). A cheerful outlook is a wonderful safety valve. It is the ability to laugh at the mistakes we make and the losses we suffer.

The ability to laugh at misfortunes is a wonderful human talent. In 1994, Mario M. Cuomo, New York governor, was defeated in his campaign for a fourth term as governor. After his defeat, Cuomo made a cheerful, tongue-in-cheek observation: "Ever since the Republican's landslide on November 8th, it's been getting dark outside a little earlier every day. You notice that?" (qtd. in Hennenberger 28). Leaders who cannot see the humor in much of what happens are likely to be dangerous to themselves and dangerous to others.

Savor Every Moment. To savor every moment is to be aware of the present. Cheerful leaders are those who recognize and appreciate what they have right now. As noted earlier, an essential part of savoring every moment is to learn to laugh at oneself. Cheerful leaders enjoy poking fun at themselves. According to news reports, the major attraction at the Clinton Presidential Library is a video of the president's appearances at the White House Correspondents'

Association dinners and other lighter moments. The video is part of the 22-minute program "A Time to Laugh" that has played at the library since it opened in 2005. This video attracts the most attention of visitors who visit the Clinton Library.

Find Humor in Frustrations. Finding humor in frustrations means to seek out the sunny side that is almost always embedded in them. As the ancient Greeks recognized, tragedy and comedy are two sides of the same coin. According to the great humorist James Thurber, "Humor is emotional chaos remembered in tranquility" (xv).

Annoying people are the bane of public officials. Before becoming president of the United States, Woodrow Wilson served as a highly popular governor of New Jersey. The story goes that during this time a close personal friend and New Jersey senator died suddenly. This was deeply troubling to Wilson. Almost immediately after he was informed of his friend's death, he received a phone call. According to the anecdote, the caller asked if he could be first in line to take the dead senator's place, to Wilson's great annoyance. Wilson replied, "That's fine with me, if the undertaker has no objections." Cheerful leaders are able to find humor even in the frustrations of dealing with fools.

Making the best of bad situations, past and present, is a hallmark of the cheerful leader. When President John F. Kennedy was asked, "How did you become a hero in World War II?" He replied, "It was easy—they sank my boat" (qtd. in Kennedy 22). After Adlai E. Stevenson, Democratic presidential nominee, was defeated in the presidential election of 1952, he commented, "A funny thing happened to me on the way to the White House!" (qtd. in Davis 292) Cheerful leaders accept the reality of bad situations, but they handle frustrations by being of good cheer.

Fight Fair. Cheerful leaders are not afraid to fight for human decency. They recognize their own rights and the rights of others. Leaders, being human, are tempted to run rough-shod over people, particularly if the have the desire and power to do so. We have all known leaders who achieve power by denying the rights of others and ignoring their feelings. However, this power can only be maintained by brute force. Such leaders often pay a high price for denying the rights of others and ignoring their feelings. A cheerful leader is one who enrolls others, voluntarily and enthusiastically, in his or her vision.

A special quality of cheerful leaders is that they follow rules of decent conduct. They are not dirty fighters. They tend to be courageous in difficult times, courteous to everyone, chivalrous toward weaker individuals, and considerate of the defeated. They win and lose gracefully.

Challenge Authority. There are times when it is necessary for cheerful leaders to challenge authority. For example, George (Herbert Walker) Bush once commented, "I do not like broccoli, and I haven't liked it since I was a kid and I am now president of the United States, and I am not going to eat anymore broccoli" (qtd. in Hines 6). As a dear friend, William Stafford, pointed out, saying no to others is a good way to say yes to ourselves.

Cheerful leaders are likely to possess a built-in "crap detector" that recognizes nonsense, arrogance, and certainty. Voltaire is credited with the comment that doubt is not a very agreeable status, but certainty is a ridiculous one.

Cheerful leaders have a special talent for sticking pins in pomposity. Good humor can often stop a snob, a bully, a pretender, or a pompous ass in his or her tracks. President Harry Truman provided an example of how to handle a challenge to his authority:

> I fired General Douglas MacArthur because he wouldn't respect the authority of the president. That's the answer to that. I didn't fire him because he was a dumb son of a bitch, although he was, but that's not against the law for generals. If it was, half to three-quarters of them would be in jail. (qtd. in Miller 287)

The bigger the balloon, the louder the pop.

Any Attempt is a Victory. The final signature strength of cheerful leaders is that they recognize that the victory is in the attempt. For them, the question is, "Did I try and fail, or did I fail to try?" There is an adage in basketball that a player misses one hundred percent of the shots he or she did not take. Any investment in living, no matter how small or in what area, has tremendous potential. The smallest action can be more significant than the largest intention.

I once had the pleasure of dining with a young athlete who had been a member of a recent United States Olympic Team. She had not won any medals. During our meal, she made a comment worth repeating here. She said, "Taking part is winning, not taking part is losing, and that's what winning and losing are all about."

Making the attempt is half the battle, but it is what many leaders fear most. Some years ago I spent some time with a school superintendent. When some suggestions for school improvement came up, he would often respond, "I can't do that; it would get me fired." He was fired anyway—because he was afraid to make improvements.

Every time I pass a graveyard, I think of all the dreams that are buried there. I reflect on all those who might have been dancers, all those who might have been singers, or poets, or artists. Many lacked the courage to try. Now they sleep in a garden of dead dreams.

Conclusion

Cheerful leaders don't take themselves too seriously. They work to savor every moment, to find humor in frustrations, to fight fair, to challenge authority, and to believe that any attempt is a victory. They are reconstructionists, as opposed to participants. They like to make things happen. As Winston Churchill explained, "I like to make things happen, and if they don't happen, I like to make them happen" (qtd. in James 207). What better description could there be of Betty Faye Siegel, coal miner's daughter and a truly cheerful leader?

Works Cited

Davis, Kenneth S. *The Politics of Honor: A Biography of Adlai Stevenson*. New York: G.P. Putnam's Sons, 1967.

Ford, Gerald. "The Friendship, and Toughness, of Hugh Sidey." Editorial. *Washington Post* 26 Nov. 2005, final ed.: A25.

Goodwin, Doris Kearns. *No Ordinary Time: Franklin and Eleanor Roosevelt: The Home Front in World War II*. New York: Touchstone-Simon & Schuster, 1995.

Henneberger, Melinda. "Cuomo Makes His Last Speech as an Official, in a Hurry." *New York Times* 17 Dec. 1994, late ed., sec.1: 28.

Hines, Cragg. "Veggie Vendetta: President Declares His Distaste for Broccoli is Irreversible." *Houston Chronicle* 23 Mar. 1990: 6.

James, Robert Rhodes. *Churchill: A Study in Failure, 1900-1939*. New York: World Publishing, 1970.

Kenney, Charles. *John F. Kennedy: The Presidential Portfolio: History as Told Through the John F. Kennedy Library and Museum*. New York: Public Affairs-Perseus Books Groups, 2000.

McCabe, John. *Mr. Laurel and Mr. Hardy: An Affectionate Biography*. 1962. New York: Doubleday, 1985.

Miller, Mark. *Plain Speaking: An Oral Biography of Harry S. Truman*. New York: Berkley Pub. Corp., 1974.

Purkey, William Watson. *Teaching Class Clowns (And What They Can Teach Us)*. Thousand Oaks: Corwin Press, 2006.

Reagan, Ronald. *An American Life: The Autobiography*. New York: Pocket-Simon & Schuster, 1990.

Seligman, Martin. *Authentic Happiness: Using the New Positive Psychology to Realize Your Potential For Lasting Fulfillment*. New York: Free Press-Simon & Schuster, 2002.

Shakespeare, William. *King Richard II: The Arden Edition of the Works of William Shakespeare*. Ed. Peter Ure. Cambridge: Harvard UP, 1956.

Divine Choreography

Ferrol Sams

I called Dr. Elizabeth Giddens.

"Tell me about this Siegelfest and what I'm supposed to write."

"Well, we're getting all sorts of things: some of them tributes to Dr. Siegel; some of them short personal pieces."

"What's the purpose of the collection?"

"Well, Dr. Siegel started out talking about spirituality and the effect certain instances of it have had on people. I'm not sure I know exactly what she means by 'spirituality.' I prefer the term 'conscientiousness.'"

I mused on this overnight.

Sometimes a series of concrete actions can, in retrospect, appear to be spiritual and have a lasting effect on a person. I am sure Dr. Siegel has experienced this many times in her vivid interactions with people. While it is happening, such an event seems the logical outcome of one's training and an automatic response to circumstance. Looking back, the events appear totally illogical and one's reaction an example of Aristotle's definition of "good."

I give you an example.

In 1951 my physician wife and I began a general practice clinic in impoverished Fayette County, Georgia, where I was a fifth-generation son. We rapidly became very busy, so busy that I had developed the habit when going on a rural house call of snatching up whichever child was wandering loose. This gave me companionship and the opportunity of imprinting on the child's consciousness that, eccentric as I might appear, I was a father.

One noon after a hurried lunch, I took second son Jim with me on a call out past the little one-room New Hope Baptist Church to check on Mr. Carl Graves, Sr. The child was a pleasure and I enjoyed visiting with him. On the way back to the office, driving south on the recently paved, two-laned State Highway 85, we passed Simpson's meat processing plant.

Mr. Simpson had bought Hoy Kirkly's Frozen Food Locker, the demand for which had declined after home freezers came on the market and a modicum of prosperity had penetrated Fayette County. Mr. Simpson converted it into a wholesale business that involved selling processed beef to grocery stores and suppliers. He hired about 20 or so meat cutters to prepare the carcasses.

As we approached the building I noticed a group of four white-suited, white-gowned, white-capped men carrying a comrade out the front door. It was five after one o'clock and I was due back at the office at one. I said to Jim, "Son, that looks like Raymond Dixon those men are carrying out. He's a patient of Daddy's and faints at the sight of blood. He's probably cut his finger and passed out."

On impulse I wheeled up to the door at Simpson's. "What's the matter?" I asked. "Raymond cut himself?"

"Yeah, Doc. We don't know where, but he was boning beef and let out a yell and passed out on the floor. We ain't seen no blood, though."

"You carrying him down to my office?"

"Yeah, soon as we get him down to the parking lot."

"Oh, open the door and put him in the back seat; I'm headed there right now and it'll save y'all a trip."

They lowered his feet into the back of my car and it sounded like someone had suddenly emptied a five-gallon bucket of water.

I looked back. Jim had scooted over to the far corner of the seat. The floor of my car was filled with bright red blood to the top of the middle hump. "Take him out!" I yelled. "Lay him flat on the ground! Get his pants down! Quick!"

I raced to the trunk, snatched out my bag and a liter of saline, knelt by Raymond in the dirt, and found the wound. It was in the groin on the left, about a half-inch long, and spurting. Despite the chain mail apron all the employees wore when boning beef, the keen tip of his boning knife had penetrated the closely-woven links and Raymond had stabbed himself.

I grabbed a pad of four-by-four gauze sponges, told one of the men to hold it as tight as he possibly could over the wound, and with frantic prayer managed to get an IV started in his left arm before every vein in his body collapsed. That was not an example of my skill; it was an answer to prayer, which is very nebulous and rarer than we like to admit.

I took over the pressure in the groin with my right fist grinding forcefully into the wound.

"Call the ambulance!" I yelled.

"We already did!"

Within minutes Harry Redwine arrived in his hearse which doubled as our only ambulance when it transported living people.

"Call my wife! Tell her to call Dr. Glass to meet us at Georgia Baptist! Call the state patrol! Tell them to block the traffic for us! Let's roll, Harry!"

I left Jim standing in his underpants on the back seat with both doors wide open and a pool of blood at his feet.

The trip into town is blurred somewhat in memory and associated with the constant whine of the sirens. I know that my hand and fist grew numb and then began aching, but I also knew I dared not lessen the pressure, not even to change fists. The IV dripped steadily. Thank you, God.

As we crossed the bridge over I-75 at Riverdale, Raymond opened his eyes. His freckles stood out like gold in the stark pallor of his face.

"Am I going to die, Sambo?"

"Most certainly not," I equivocated firmly. "Everything's under control and we'll be at the hospital in a very few minutes."

"I hope not," he whispered.

"So do I," I thought silently.

Dr. Glass and a whole covey of attendants awaited us. Within minutes type O blood was being pumped into both Raymond's arms and his right leg.

"Whatever you do, Sambo, don't move your fist; we have the operating room ready. Let's go." He was very calm.

In the OR my fist was also cleaned and prepped in the middle of the operating field with green soap and iodine.

The anesthesiologist said, "Doctor, I cannot put this man to sleep; he is in shock."

Dr. Glass forsook his calm. "He's never going to get out of shock unless we operate. If you're not going to put him to sleep, get off that goddam stool and I'll get somebody who will! And I'll tend to you later!"

Within seconds the Pentothal was working.

"Now, Sambo, be very still. I'm going to have to cut around your fist."

A few minutes later he had a bulldog clamp around the vessel, proximal to the wound.

"I'll be blessed! He got the common iliac. I can't believe he didn't bleed to death. You can move your fist now."

That's what he thought. I had to take my left hand and lift my fist out of the operating field. It was hours before I had any feeling in it.

I made my way to the waiting room, drained emotionally, exhausted physically, and craving a cigarette.

I was accosted by Raymond's old-maid aunt who was the ruling dragon of the family. She had a political job at the state capitol and had rushed over to the hospital to take command. Her subjugated relatives were cowering in the corner.

I have never been comfortable with imperious women who close their eyes while they are speaking directly to me, a most annoying, albeit effective, method of demanding attention. You don't dare let your gaze stray lest they open those eyes unexpectedly. Without inquiring how Raymond was faring, she addressed me, "Sambo, tell these doctors I want no expense spared to save Raymond's life." She opened her eyes briefly, then shut them again. "And if he needs blood I want you to see to it that he gets it."

What a wonderful lightning rod. I immediately felt re-energized, confirmed, and deliciously annoyed.

"Not to worry, Vivian, he's already had eight pints and no one has even considered expense. Now, where is his wife? She's the one I want to talk to."

I turned as she closed her eyes again and spoke before Vivian could. "Patsy, the artery is sewed up; Dr. Glass has done a wonderful job. Raymond's blood pressure is 120/80 and he's going to be fine. Let's get back to Fayetteville, Harry."

I dreaded cleaning up my car. Jim, bless his heart, had grown weary of looking at all the blood and had very carefully layered the pages of the *Constitution,* page after page, over both sides of the floor before a solicitous neighbor had carried him home to his mother. The blood had soaked into the porous paper and clotted firmly to it. All I had to do was slide it out and the rubber mat beneath was easily sponged.

Now.

There is no doubt that this event affected me spiritually. It certainly affected Raymond that way. He has a circular scar in his left groin to reinforce it. We are both grateful to God.

Raymond thinks I saved his life.

I do not.

Something greater than I was involved that day. Call it chance. Call it the Higher Force acknowledged by AA. Call it God's will. Even say that the King of Hebron shall know there is a prophet in Israel. Call it what you will: It remains a highlight and a turning point in my life. In my mind, it is more spiritual than physical. "Here am I, Lord. Send me."

What if? What if Mr. Carl Graves had not needed a house call? I would not have been on Highway 85 at 1:00 p.m.

What if I had not on a whim turned into Simpson's parking lot? Raymond would have exsanguinated before they got him to my office.

What if Harry Redwine had been away from home? Or Dr. Glass had not been available? Or the state patrol had not been Johnny-on-the-spot?

Helen Elliott, founder of Peachtree Publishers, was somewhat of a mystic, and she spoke often with quiet and beautiful assurance of "divine choreography and the confluence of events." I associate her with the definition of "spirituality."

When I first met Dr. Betty Siegel with her great big round, red-rimmed glasses, I thought momentarily of a hoot owl with a hangover.

It did not take long, however, for me to become aware of deep wellsprings of life force in this extremely gifted and compassionate woman. She reinforces my impulse to acknowledge the spiritual side of humans equally with their intellectual ability.

Look at her.

Look at her accomplishments.

Conscientiousness? Yes. I'll grant Dr. Giddens that much.

Spirituality? Most definitely, and it's easier to spell.

Divine choreography? Absolutely! Helen Elliott was right.

Confluence of events involving many people? You bet! Look at the lives she has touched.

She has it all.

You go, Betty!

"Harvard in the Pines": A Reminiscence

Howard Shealy

You and I have a number of things in common, Betty Faye: our rural southern roots; our long enterprise working with so many others to grow a small junior college, barely out of its junior college days, into an outstanding regional university; our love of travel and the arts; and above all, our love of teaching. You have always said that you regarded teaching as a "calling." To my mind as a historian, the word "calling" simultaneously suggests the Catholic concept of a vocation, the Calvinist notion that each of us has a role to play in the divine schema that must be carried out with the utmost diligence, and the Renaissance humanist belief that we all have innate talents that should be developed to their fullest if we are to be personally fulfilled and are to contribute fully to society. You also frequently remind us at commencements and convocations that all of us who are engaged in the academic enterprise are teachers, no matter what our official titles, because everything we do is ultimately derived from our collective purpose of educating our students and our community.

As I look back on nearly 30 years as a member of the faculty at Kennesaw State, I can certainly identify with the idea of being "called to teach," and I thank you for having made the connection for me between the activity I find most fulfilling and the remembered notion from my rural past of those who were "called to preach." In April 2005, I was unexpectedly hospitalized for cardiac by-pass surgery. Friends and colleagues who came to visit while I was undergoing preliminary tests and waiting for the scheduled surgery were surprised to find me reading student research papers and organizing the selection of the next year's study abroad faculty for Italy by telephone. They should not have been. What did they expect I would be doing with my enforced idleness? This continuation of my obligations to my students, both those currently in my class and those who would participate in study abroad a year later, was something I had been conditioned to from my earliest days at Kennesaw College. It was what the notion of a calling demanded. It was the kind of thing you would have been doing yourself. It was the kind of behavior and the kind of attitude you had encouraged by precept and example from the day you assumed the presidency of that little college we old-timers called "Harvard in the Pines."

As you know, I arrived at Kennesaw College a few years before you did. In 1978, I was part of the first wave of new hires to support the twelve-year-old junior college's transition to four-year status. I did not recognize any feeling of being "called to teach" at the time. A hungry young PhD, recently graduated from Emory University, I did not even have the good sense to ask President Sturgis what my starting salary would be before I accepted the position. I was just too elated at my good fortune to even think about the money. It was a real, tenure-track job at a four-year college at a time when many of my contemporaries despaired of ever finding such a position. Kennesaw College soon became a home, a community, and a calling, however.

I arrived with very little teaching experience: one class in Western Civilization at Emory. At Kennesaw, I would be teaching three classes each quarter that included Asian and African history as well as the familiar West. I remember feeling inadequate to the task before me and seeking advice from my major professor, George Cuttino. I was so acutely aware of how much I did not know even after all my years of undergraduate and graduate study. "Don't worry," he reassured me, "no one ever really knows history until he teaches it. Then you will have to learn it because your students will demand it of you." Soon I discovered I had some talent for teaching. According to my student evaluations, even in those early years, I could do it pretty well, in fact. Above all, I discovered that I loved it. I could not believe I was getting paid for doing something that gave me so much satisfaction, so much pure pleasure.

For my first decade at Kennesaw, I shared an office with J.B. Tate, a charter member of the junior college faculty and one of the best classroom teachers I have ever known. Yes, we were short of office space and resources even from the outset. There was no formal mentoring program for new faculty, but we made a virtue of necessity. Shared offices meant shared experiences and shared wisdom between generations of dedicated teachers. We believed that we could not always wait for the resources to come to us: We had a mission to accomplish and a constantly growing student population to serve.

In those days, faculty joked about teaching at "Harvard in the Pines." Perhaps it was partly an attempt to cover our own sense of being the "new kid" in the academic world of the Georgia university system or the sense of being geographically remote from the heart of Atlanta, but it also captured the spirit of what we were about. Those early faculty members and the administrators who hired them inaugurated a proud tradition of teaching excellence that has been the hallmark of Kennesaw State ever since. We were definitely, literally, in the pines. All traces of the Frey family farm had vanished by 1978, but as I drove north to the campus along I-75, there was nothing to see but huge thickets of pine trees. Nothing stood at the junction of the interstate highway and Chastain Road except the campus and the now venerable Waffle House. We were set down in our own little corner of still undeveloped Cobb County, the only four-year public college outside the Perimeter.

In those early years of Kennesaw College, we were hard at work developing degree programs and preparing our first majors for graduation and careers, though many of our students still thought of us as a way station where they completed their core requirements before transferring to Georgia State or the University of Georgia. We were proud of what we were doing, but our vision was still limited to creating a "fine little college" where students could earn a four-year degree as solid as any offered outside the flagship universities in the Georgia system and the more elite private universities in the metro area.

There are moments when one can sense a shift in the cosmos. So it was in our little world of Harvard in the Pines when you arrived as the new president. I distinctly remember President Sturgis' decision to retire, indeed many faculty saw it as a passing of the Old Guard that was overdue. I remember the excitement of the search for a new president and your acceptance. I especially remember my colleague, Fred Roach, who chaired the committee for your inauguration and his anxiety that everything should be done absolutely properly from the issuing of invitations to the ordering of the inauguration procession. We all knew "something big" was happening when you came to Kennesaw College. Little did we imagine how much change we would all experience together over the next 25 years. We could not have imagined then the phenomenal growth in enrollment from just over 4,000 students at your arrival to more than 18,000 now. Nor could we have envisioned the physical growth the campus has seen in buildings and facilities. The transformation in the institution itself has been the most astonishing of all. With your leadership, however, we have remained true to the soul, the core mission of Harvard in the Pines: the calling to teach.

In a recent interview with the *Atlanta Journal-Constitution* about your career at KSU, you said that you did not want to be remembered for buildings, but the change in the appearance and feel of the campus since those early days is truly remarkable. The campus I knew in 1978, which was almost identical to the junior college campus, is hidden in a corner and sits in the shadow of all that has come since. Only the Social Science Building retains its original identity, and even as I write this, it is about to be replaced by the largest, most technologically advanced and environmentally efficient classroom building on campus. The Carmichael Student Center, still known as the "new student center" when you and I first came to Kennesaw, has been absorbed by its much larger successor. The junior college library is now the Pilcher Building. The School of Nursing occupies a totally renovated Science Building, and so forth. We have been good stewards of place, continually recycling the original fabric of the campus even as demands and missions have changed. The number of new buildings that have arisen on the Frey property since your arrival would have been beyond our wildest imaginings in 1978. You dedicated the Sturgis Library shortly after your arrival. Then came the Humanities Building, the first truly new classroom building. (I still mourn the pink dogwood that grew on the site, which was visible from the window of my first office.) The Burruss Building, the Wilson Building and Stillwell Theater, Science and Mathematics, the Clendenin Building, and Kennesaw Hall all rose from the red clay in a dizzying succession. We finally escaped the last vestiges of our junior college past with the opening of the first student residences in 2002 and of Convocation Hall in 2005. The new Social Science Building is scheduled to be dedicated in 2007, and ground has been broken for the new performance hall. Pine trees have steadily given way to a truly impressive university campus.

In addition to, and more important than, buildings, however, you brought us a vision of what we could be. You inspired us to see ourselves and the possibilities before us in new ways, starting with the View of the Future project chaired by Helen Ridley in 1981-1982. You challenged us to think beyond our cozy self-concept of being a very good, small, suburban college with a core of bright faculty serving a largely local, non-traditional student population and sending an exceptional few of our best and brightest graduates on to graduate programs at the kinds of universities where we had earned our own PhDs. You embraced our commitment to teaching and our emphasis on community service, but you challenged us to think in terms of innovative new degree and certificate programs and to expand our service commitment to the entire Northwest Crescent of Georgia and even into the international arena.

We began our graduate programs with career-oriented, high-demand degrees like business administration, education, and nursing. We soon carved out our own special niches within the USG with innovative, cohort-based programs like the Executive MBA and the Master's in Conflict Management and in Public Administration. Who would have dreamed in 1981 that we would regularly offer a cohort-based M.P.A. for mid-level administrators from the People's Republic of China? Your openness to all possibilities allowed us to think in those terms and to make the vision a reality.

Our international connection to China was not our first, but it has been one of the longest and most productive of all the international relationships you fostered by establishing faculty exchanges and partnerships with universities around the globe. One of your earliest initiatives in this area was the creation of the International Programs Center, which was charged with coordinating all our international efforts from the "Year of a Country" programs begun in 1984-1985 to study abroad and faculty exchanges. Beginning with the Year of Japan, the country study series offered innovative courses for our students, an outstanding series of guest speakers for the campus and community, and artistic exhibitions and performances. Each program generally culminated with a group trip to the country or region that had been the focus of the year's activities. The realization that these trips were often the first international travel experience for some of our faculty, even those who taught world history, art, or literature, is yet another measure of how much we have changed in the past 25 years. The number of faculty who travel abroad to present their work at international conferences, to participate in faculty development experiences sponsored by the Fulbright foundation and others, and to teach in study abroad grows every year.

The growth in the number of students and faculty participating in study abroad has been truly phenomenal. We began with a handful of students and one or two faculty in Mexico, first at San Miguel and then at Oaxaca. As we added partners and international contacts, our programs have expanded to include Western Europe from Oxford to St. Petersburg, much of the Americas and the Caribbean, Asia, and Africa. By 2005, KSU offered about 25 programs in 20 different countries with around 300 students and 20 faculty participating.

I still have the fondest memories of traveling with you and Joel in Italy in 2001. We walked the ancient streets of Rome together (and sometimes explored beneath them), lunched and tasted wines at a Tuscan castle, and experienced the splendors of Renaissance Florence. The best moment, however, was when the students arrived for our study-abroad program in tiny Montepulciano. You were so excited to see them, and they to see you there. You visited their classes at the Medici fortress, chatted with them over cappuccinos in Café Poliziano, and took the kind of interest in who they were and what they were learning from their study-abroad experience that I find hard to conceive in any other university president. You were fully "in the moment" with those students and their learning. The program in Montepulciano is a good example of how we have grown as an institution in our efforts to provide global learning experiences for our students. It has grown from 24 students from the entire university system at its inception to 107 last summer, and we still maintain a waiting list every year.

While more of our students and faculty have experienced international travel over the years, the world has simultaneously been coming to us in a steadily increasing flow. We now have some 1,600 international students from more than 130 countries, and virtually every academic department in the university boasts one or more international faculty members. More remarkable still, those students come to us, not because of any concerted effort to recruit them but because of the attraction of our location and the reputation Kennesaw State has established in their home countries and/or among their contacts in the United States. Our recently established new major in African and African Diaspora Studies is unique in the state, and I believe in the region, in encompassing both the tradition of African American studies and the global diaspora of peoples of African origin. We have become, as you like to say, Georgia's International University where the inclusion of international students and faculty, international travel and study opportunities, and international themes in our academic programs is the norm rather than the exception. This transformation would not have taken place without your leadership, and it is clearly acknowledged in the elevation of the International Programs Center into the Institute for Global Initiatives and the selection of "global learning for all" as the theme for our Quality Enhancement Plan for SACS for the coming five years.

Just as we have experienced tremendous growth in the size of the student body and in campus facilities, our faculty has also experienced a transformation in the course of your presidency. We "long marchers" were proud of who we were, and rightly so, but we were a largely homogeneous group. Most of us were graduates of the University of Georgia, Georgia State, and Emory. Virtually all of us came from universities in the South. We poured our energies into the building of the four-year degree programs, into service to the community, and into giving our students the best education we could deliver. There was only a limited focus on scholarship in those early days, and financial support for research was virtually non-existent. In a recent interview for PBS, you noted that we have added the equivalent of an entire new faculty every five or six years at KSU for the past two decades. These new colleagues have added immensely to the strength, the depth, and the diversity of Kennesaw State. In my own department, in the past three years, we have hired new faculty whose PhDs are from Wisconsin, Michigan, UCLA, and Yale. Our most recent new colleagues come from as far away as China and Liberia. Almost all of them come to us with an established research program, often with their first book in hand or nearing completion. As my father would have said, they "hit the ground running" when they arrived at KSU, presenting at top academic conferences around the world, publishing in prestigious presses and journals, and, in the process, establishing a name for themselves and enhancing the reputation of our university.

At the same time, they are dedicated teachers who can spin a tale from history as well as any of us old-timers while they make effective use of the latest classroom technology designed to fire the imaginations of a new generation of students. They are just as excited as we were 25 and 30 years ago about building for the future. As I interview candidates for new positions, I tell each of them about the exciting possibilities that lie before them. Those of us who came on board when Kennesaw College really was in the pines had the chance to build a four-year college and its programs. Those who are joining our ranks now will have the opportunity to transform a strong and proud regional university into a truly great institution with national and even international recognition.

They would not have such an unparalleled opportunity— Kennesaw State would not have become what it is—without your dedication and leadership over the past 25 years. The university certainly would have seen enrollment growth, just as our sister institutions West Georgia and Clayton State have, though it is not at all clear that we would have seen the dynamic growth we have experienced without the recognition you have brought to the institution with your publications, conferences, and unbelievable number of public appearances. Most important, you brought us your vision, your sense that all things really are possible if we want them badly enough. You brought us the drive to be and do more, even in the face of limited resources. Your sense that you and the university shared a "calling" resonated with those of us who were already here, and together we have managed to communicate it to each of the "new faculties" who have joined us every half-decade.

In commencement addresses you often note that the word *alumni* (foster sons or daughters) comes from the Latin *alere* which means "to nourish." Likewise, *alma mater* or "foster mother" is drawn from Latin words that evoke the rearing and training of the next generation. That imagery of nourishing and foster parenthood comes to my mind when I think of the careers that you and I and others have spent at Kennesaw State. We have nourished generations of foster sons and daughters intellectually and spiritually and prepared them to lead rich and productive lives. We have taught them that learning does not stop with the attainment of a degree, or even a series of degrees, and we have tried to make them "good stewards of place" whether that means preserving historic heritage, the natural environment, or human rights. To my mind, however, the processes of nourishing and parenting apply to us and to the university as well, and the relationship is symbiotic. In one sense, all of us owe a tremendous amount to Kennesaw State. She has nourished us and given us careers with purpose. At the same time, we are the original generation of shapers who made the institution what she has become so far, and yours has been the master vision. As a child psychologist who has seen her two sons grow up and establish their own families and careers, you must also look with pride on KSU, your "foster daughter," as she moves from adolescence towards maturity. In spite of the dizzying growth in enrollment, the new buildings, and the constant expansion of our mission, you have helped her and us maintain one constant principle. The soul of the university has remained dedicated to our calling, providing the best environment for teaching and learning possible. Those of us who have been here longest are best positioned to appreciate just how remarkable that is, and we know that it would not have been possible had you not shared that same sense of calling.

One of the ways you have often summed up your gratitude to the founders of Kennesaw State is by saying, "I drink from a well I did not dig." The same thing will be said by students, faculty, and administrators generations from now if they are truly aware of the institution's history. The well from which they will drink will be fed not only from an ancient spring that flows from Harvard in the Pines but by a multitude of channels opened in the years in which you presided over the university's growth and development. In conclusion, I would like to add the comments of two recent graduates to my own reminiscences about "the Siegel years" at Kennesaw State.

Dr. Siegel has provided a much-needed role model for women in education. In academia, one often sees a slew of male faces with a peppering of female faces for variety. Dr. Siegel's long, illustrious career exemplifies the impact that women can have in academia. Personally, I am grateful for my time at Kennesaw State University and the positive image that Dr. Siegel provided.

Rosemary McClellan,
B.A. in History, 2004

I have been fortunate to learn at this university. Not only is that faculty brilliant and challenging, but there is also an atmosphere of caring and concern for student success outside of professors' individual classes. Betty Siegel has cultivated this campuswide attitude with her words and actions. Her constant interaction with students and requests for personal, one-on-one feedback demonstrate the high value she places on student experience. President Siegel has helped shape a university with student success, academic and otherwise, at its core.

Amanda McNary,
B.A. in History, 2006

Balancing Public and Private Selves: In Search of the Mean

David J. Siegel

Very well, says the junior partner. You can have me at work. I will do the things you command, however unsavory, and I will try to remember my place at all times. You are the master, and I am your humble servant, at least within these confines. But I will build a parallel universe full of wondrous beauty where things grow freely, and this place will serve as my sanctuary. This garden universe I will build just off the deck in my backyard, with a little help from my good friends at the Home Depot.

A man gives money to a homeless person. The man's friends observe that this act of charity is quite out of character, and they wonder aloud (and a little mockingly) if his heart is softening. In fact, this is exactly what is happening, but the object of his compassion is not the homeless person to whom he has just made the transfer. He may be only dimly aware that the gesture is actually atonement for an incident several weeks earlier in which he berated a hapless customer service representative over some embarrassingly trivial matter.

We cheat our bosses daily, and we mean to. Our thoughts wander; we take a newspaper to the washroom where we linger for an extra five minutes to catch up on world events; we keep talismanic objects or photos within easy reach and use them as escape hatches into a fantasy world far away from the present circumstances. We also cheat our families; we think about work when we're playing ball with the kids, and the residue of work problems clings to us even when we're on vacation. In this way, meanderings on company time are compensated for by doubling back around to workaday concerns when we're on our own time.

———⇒•⊂———

In each of these vignettes, there is a force of balance at work, however vague and circuitous. We build monuments to balance, some of them actual and physical, some of them floating on air. There may or may not be one-to-one correspondence between cause and effect; the garden in the first vignette may grow in tandem with workplace slights, but guilt works in mysterious ways to steer the man in the second vignette toward a redemptive encounter. The scenario described in the third vignette ultimately redounds to the benefit of both employee and employer, but interrupting the cycle at any point would create a disadvantage for one or the other party, so round and round it goes.

Let me put forward a proposition and a disclaimer. The proposition is that balance is our project. The disclaimer is that I am not specially qualified to hold forth on the subject; I certainly profess no expertise in matters of balance, except that I participate with the rest of humanity in an epic struggle to get it right, which entails plenty of experimentation but little in the way of definitive solutions. What follows, then, is more of a meditation (and a tentative one at that) than an instructive blueprint or a guide to action.

Balance is what we, as individuals, seek in our own lives, but it is also the condition to which our whole ecosystem aspires and is calibrated. Our situation ultimately tends toward balance, though daily forces often seem to conspire against it. Considerations of balance are central to the decisions we make, the actions we take, and the ideas we generate. It is the undercurrent of our human and societal strivings. We will go to extraordinary lengths to achieve balance, including creating alternative lifeworlds in our heads or in works of art. Where there is disorder, let us impose order and control. Where there is ugliness, let us impart some aesthetic quality. But it also works the other way around. Where there is too much order and control, let us disrupt. Where there is too much attention to beauty, let us confront the grotesque and perverse. Thesis needs antithesis. Balance, after all, is our aim.

One of our greatest challenges, and one made more pressing by globalization and disappearing boundaries, is to live in harmony with the other and otherness, whether "the other" is taken to mean the component parts of oneself, other people, ideas, entire systems, or civilizations. It is messy and delicate work, and there is no template or accredited process to chart the course. Every day, there are countless modifications that have to be made just to get along in the world. At base, we subordinate self-interest for the good of some collective enterprise. That is difficult enough. But we also slip into and out of a host of different roles—parent, child, worker, neighbor, consumer, member, and so on—with the agility and dexterity of a stage actor. Sometimes, there is a marvel of simultaneity at work in our lives, and all of our affairs and commitments seem to complement each other in both cosmic and practical ways. (Synergy delights us, because there is a certain element of efficiency in it, as well as a sense of spiritual oneness.) Other times, we feel stretched in many disparate directions, and the imbalance provokes rage or frustration or confusion. In our attempt to pull it all together, we lock horns with powerful centrifugal forces in our midst.

The Divided Self

Modern society is dominated by norms of rationality, bureaucracy, and specialization. This is an ancient condition, as old as organization itself. In the *Metamorpheses*, Ovid described the transformation of the universe from "rude and lumpy matter" (3) to a neatly ordered, well-functioning, and demarcated system. With the rise of science and technology and the encroachment of business logic into non-business domains, the situation has only become more pronounced. In her 1979 book *Women and Dualism*, sociologist Lynda Glennon outlined the net effect of escalating scientism, technocracy, and expertism: the division and subdivision of self. The unique requirements of our variegated roles, in other words, have catalyzed a form of compartmentalization and fragmentation that effectively separates us from ourselves and induces something like personality disorder. Glennon presents the idea of an instrumental-expressive duality at work in our lives, with instrumentalism representing qualities typically associated with purposive action and expressivism capturing the realm of emotion. The instrumental-expressive dichotomy is roughly equivalent to head-heart, reason-passion, and public-private distinctions. Drawing on social thought that extends back to Marx and Weber, Glennon observes that modern technological society is overwhelmed by an instrumental ethos.

We don't need social thinkers, though, to tell us what our personal experience plainly confirms: Some of the most intimate aspects of our lives are being conducted, regulated, or "improved" by technology or outsourced to experts. Charity, compassion, sexual performance, emotional feeling, and even imagination—the instruments of modern society claim to do these better or more efficiently than we can ourselves. We have charitable organizations that accept and distribute funds, essentially functioning as "middle men" that depersonalize the experience by disconnecting givers and receivers. As pernicious and conspiratorial as it sounds, we have even mechanized the means through which we do our own thinking (that most human of endeavors); the critic Curtis White has suggested that too much of our creativity has been turned over to a giant media apparatus (movies, television, radio) that acts like "an imagination prosthetic" for us. The impulse to achieve wholeness may be a protectionist reaction against such entropy. Connectedness, integration, reunification, balance—these are related constructs that, on one level, are meant to neutralize forces of fragmentation.

Our lives are lived in public spaces, in all kinds of organizations (family, school, neighborhoods, corporations, and so on). We are called upon to play different roles, and we become role specialists; this doesn't just happen in our jobs, it happens in every area of our lives. Sometimes, the qualities required for the effective discharge of our duties in one role (an instrumental approach at work, for example) are antithetical to the conduct of our other roles (such as providing emotional support to the family). Clearly, tension between these roles (role conflict) is the result, and seepage is likely to occur, sometimes with positive effects and sometimes with negative ones. Keeping tight boundaries between different spheres of life may win praise from an employer, but it can be soul-destroying for its practitioner.

We "contain multitudes" (51.9), as Walt Whitman famously proclaimed, and yet these can become obstructed or neglected in the course of a lifetime as we capitulate to the demands of the social structure. Consistency is what is prized in public life; the riotous confederation of selves must be quieted. Matthew Arnold lamented the buried life in a poignant poem of that same name, and it is a tragedy we all experience in the form of scuttled dreams, submerged parts of ourselves, or other such losses that are either foisted upon us (by, for example, the dehumanizing effects of life in organizations) or that we simply find expedient for purposes of making our way in civil society. Excavating and resurrecting these selves sometimes requires heroic effort or a turn of events.

It takes a serious illness, for example, for Andre Gide's protagonist in *The Immoralist* to embark on a journey of self-discovery and reinvention in which he comes to loosen attachments to former commitments. A scholar by temperament and training, Michel's near-death experience engenders a powerful craving for direct engagement in the world, one unmediated by text or simulacra. He vows to recover

> the man whom everything around—books, teachers, family, and I myself—had tried from the first to suppress. And I had already glimpsed him, faint,

> obscured by their encrustations, but all the more
> valuable, all the more urgent. I scorned henceforth that
> secondary, learned being whom education had pasted
> over him. Such husks had to be stripped away. (51)

This is his new manifesto (among other things, a declaration of independence from the stranglehold of "culture, propriety, rules" [146] so that he operates with near total disregard for his previous moral and intellectual indoctrination), but it is also a reversal of an earlier course, a corrective. Michel's affliction is one familiar to us all—how do we carve out our authentic fullness in a life governed by norms, expectations, conventions, and real and imagined constraints? For Michel, the tactile pleasure of being unbridled in nature, of making himself vulnerable to its risks and dangers, is full of exhilaration. He clandestinely slips out of his house at night:

> Outside—oh, I could have shouted with pleasure! What
> would I do now? I didn't even know. The sky, overcast
> all day, was cleared of its clouds; the nearly full moon
> glowed. I walked at random, without purpose, without
> desire, without constraint. I looked at everything
> with fresh eyes, lay in wait for each noise with more
> attentive ears; I savored the moisture of the night; I
> rested my hand among things; I prowled. (153)

The full force of this simple act can only be understood in the context of circumstances that drive Michel to venture out in the first place; his nighttime roaming is a grand juxtaposition to scholarly detachment, restraint, and the feebleness occasioned by illness. He is getting his other senses involved. He is, in other words, evening things out.

Finding Ourselves

The fact that Michel gets his kicks at night is apt. It is often by cover of darkness, where we are uncensored and undetected by the imperial gaze of the public eye, that we achieve our fullest flowering and sense of wholeness. I have long been fascinated by the prospect that the best (or most honest or interesting) parts of people are reserved for backstage or underground, far from the madding crowd. I imagine scenarios in which people labor furiously in a hole-and-corner way on projects of immense personal gravity to balance things out before the sun comes up—amateur poets honing their craft in stolen moments, autodidacts reading up on some arcane subject for personal edification rather than a credential, gardeners carving out little oases of beauty and order in direct proportion to the chaos and lack of control they experience at work, late nights spent pursuing disorganized pleasures and enthusiasms, all in an attempt to do the self-actualizing that eludes them in their day jobs or in other areas of their lives. If we are unfaithful to our true passions during the day and occasionally overcome with disappointment at having forsaken them, perhaps there is a stealthy nighttime version of ourselves that swoops in to save the day. This is just another way of saying that we are not defined by our careers, but the notion also emphasizes the personal agency involved in changing imperfect or unsatisfying circumstances—taking control of the situation and not relying on social institutions to do the work of fulfillment for us.

It is difficult not to conceive of this arrangement as a rebellion of sorts, and that is perhaps part of its allure. We may cast what we do as an act of defiance against the impersonal forces that would diminish us or require us to conform to some staid and bloodless regimen. Perhaps these thousands of tiny tilts at the windmill serve to buck us up and make us solid, well-adjusted communitarians ready to take our place on the public stage each day. These are ways we renew and refresh and reinvent ourselves—the lengths we go to in an effort to claim authenticity in a world and workplace that are constantly demanding "publicness" of us.

Some of my favorite characters in literature strike this kind of balance in amusing ways. Saul Bellow's aggrieved title character in the book *Herzog* writes a series of angry missives (that he never mails) to people with whom he has some quarrel. It serves the purpose of restoring balance—finding an outlet for venom that needs some place to go but would be too toxic if it were actually showered on someone. Similarly, the professor Jim Dixon in Kingsley Amis's *Lucky Jim* practices balancing techniques to hilarious effect as a sort of pre-emptive strike. Before being called into a senior professor's office for what he thinks will be a reproachful word, Jim curses liberally under his breath "so that he'd be in credit, as it were" (81) once the unpleasantness begins. (Clearly, there are times when major tilts at the windmill—not minor and imperceptible ones—are called for, and then we have civil rights movements and human rights crusades and the like. These involve the mobilization and organization of people of collective consciousness, a *group* of individuals seeking change to a system that is unjust in some way, the societal equivalent of achieving balance.)

If we lack the fortitude (or selfishness) to pursue a private agenda in the style of Gide's Michel, we can at least exult in his exploits and participate in them vicariously. One of the attractions of art and literature, to be sure, is that they facilitate entry into entirely new realms of being—they allow us to imagine circumstances differently or transcend time and place. Saul Bellow's protagonist in *Dangling Man* said of a growing book collection that had quickly outpaced his ability to consume it,

> But as long as they surrounded me they stood as guarantors of an extended life, far more precious and necessary than the one I was forced to lead daily. If it was impossible to sustain this superior life at all times, I could at least keep its signs within reach. When it became tenuous, I could see and touch them. (10)

(Note how Bellow's character must retreat into a world of books to feel more alive, while Gide's Michel must reject them in order to achieve the same outcome.)

Like art and literature, the world of ideas offers succor and the promise of a bigger existence. The key feature of ideas is the sheer limitlessness of them. This is not true of life outside the mind, where commitments and obligations, responsibilities, laws, customs, and understandings act as curbs, as they properly should. (Imagine a world in which all ideas spontaneously took form without being filtered through the prisms of rectitude and propriety. It would be our undoing.) Ideas don't have to be practical, they don't have to be functional. They can be whimsical, outlandish, offensive, dangerous, and absurd. Occasionally, some of the more temperate of these make it into the public domain to touch other people or communities, but they will have been shaped and packaged for public consumption by then. Raw ideas require no allocation of resources (at least not in the conventional monetary or physical sense), they are portable, and they are completely unregulated. They provide the ultimate refuge. The "few cubic centimeters inside your skull" (27) (to use George Orwell's phrasing) become a vast playground or laboratory for entertaining alternatives and opposites and inconsistencies, a safe haven for wildly experimental flights of fancy. The point here is that there is a place—one of our own fashioning—where we can range as freely and completely as we like.

Idea play is a wonderfully consequence-free way to live large, but there are times when our private thoughts burst their containers and potentially cause injury to those in our orbit. Sometimes we even *intend* to be hurtful, but it's a sure bet that remorse will follow. Consider displays of rage. The angry frequent flyer unleashes a torrent of obscenities when informed by the young woman behind the lost baggage counter that his suitcase seems to have missed a connecting flight. For her part, the young woman maintains composure in the face of this abuse and humiliation (perhaps thinking of the sunnier climes suggested by the destination posters that line her workspace —"Fly the Friendly Skies"...*to an island far away from this lunatic!*). The red-faced customer is unapologetic; he views his tirade as consolation for being inconvenienced. He may walk away and feel immediately contrite. More likely, though, the feeling will act as a time-release capsule and open only on contact with some future object of sympathy. He may practice what appears to be a random act of kindness (as the bumper sticker enjoins us to do), giving a fistful of dollars to the grizzled fellow in the median at a traffic light. The casual observer would never know that the action had its genesis in the ugly scene back at the lost baggage counter some days earlier.

It is too much to suggest that we should be thankful for cruelty when we see it, but we might understand it more fully as kindness in the making. Things cannot be undone per se, but they *can* be mitigated. The possibilities implied in this formulation should be an abiding source of hopefulness. If one understands the imperative of balance as a lifetime project, where actions and commitments loosely attach to their opposites across a time spectrum, then much of our judgment should be reserved until the available evidence is in. Moral virtue, according to Aristotle, is the presence of the mean— an intermediate position between excess and deficiency. There is no reason the intermediate position has to be achieved all at once, though. It can be about making up now for something excessive or deficient—something extreme—in earlier times so that *on balance* one's life is solidly in the mean.

A Clean, Well-Lighted Place to Indulge My Selves

There is another way to think about all of this, and it can be summed up in a well-worn dictum: Things are rarely as they appear. Simplicity is a fiction (but a comfortable and necessary one); there is always much more complexity lurking beneath the surface than we are typically willing to acknowledge—or able to appreciate— in a world of short attention spans. People and moments have complicated stories; every text has several subtexts. If much of public life is about simplifying and ordering things (making them more manageable, smoothing over differences, forcing wily phenomena into prefabricated scripts and categories), then there ought to be settings in which we can be fascinated or confounded by complexity without treating it as a problem to be solved. I take that as one of the chief purposes of the university. At their best, institutions of higher education encourage forays into the world of ideas. It is an agreeable environment for me, at least until further notice. Place matters; organizations—their cultures, their purposes, their effects—matter. I happen to find myself in fortunate alignment with the organization—the university —where I now spend a fair amount of my time studying organizations.

It is hard to imagine a more salutary setting for the public exercise of a divided mind. Here, in the academy, we have the luxury of getting our students to engage in thought experiments whose outcomes may have no place in the realm of practical affairs; in other words, we get to make messes that we don't have to clean up. We question certain assumptions and received wisdom. We consider it our professional responsibility to cultivate independent and critical minds, ones capable of grasping ambiguity and paradox. For example, I try to get my students to recognize that organizations both ennoble and enfeeble, that they are at once instruments of oppression and opportunity. The point is not to come down on one side or the other but to leaven accounts that would portray organizations as either uniformly this or that. Organizations, like the people who comprise them, are double. This is as true for universities as it is for other kinds of organizations.

One of the attractions of studying organizations is the opportunity to explore themes of balance played out on a small stage. Organizations are microcosms of wider social phenomenon, captive settings in which to examine the age-old tension between individual and community interests. In every organization, there is the issue of conformity to the group versus private wishes and desires. Civil society depends, of course, on rules and conventions to keep things running smoothly, and organizations are no exception. But individual preferences do not always accord with these strictures. No surprise there. The reaction produces all manner of mavericks, misfits, and malcontents. People bring their complex personal lives into organizations and other social settings. How could it be otherwise? That people can compartmentalize their lives as well as they do for the sake of some larger purpose is a triumph of the human spirit. The fact that they must is one of the tyrannies of organization. The act of reconciling these different directional pulls is perhaps the supreme task of the individual *in* the organization, resulting in a daily drama to resolve the tension.

These same patterns of balance hold true at the macro level, too. Social institutions seek balance; corporations wish to serve as instruments of social and environmental sustainability, and universities launch multi-billion dollar capital campaigns. The appetite for balance propels organizations into each other's domains. Organizations occasionally enter into partnership in order to achieve balance, and the resultant linkage produces a clash of cultures or a collision of world views. But it also generates a new hybrid form, a synthesis of formerly distinct parts. It is as if there is a wholesale obliteration of categories underway; we exist in a state of fluidity, not fixity.

Very well, say I. I will conclude my task here, for I have been long at it. These pages have boxed me in, and I must confess that I feel a little naked before you, dear reader. Don't mind me while I work my way toward the margin and out of sight for a bit. My private self is beseeching me to put a lid on it already.

Works Cited

Amis, Kingsley. *Lucky Jim*. 1954. New York: Penguin, 1992.

Bellow, Saul. *Dangling Man*. New York: Vanguard, 1944

---. *Herzog*. 1964. New York: Penguin, 1976.

Gide, Andre. *The Immoralist.* Trans. Richard Howard. New York: Vintage Books, 1970.

Glennon, Lynda M. *Women and Dualism: A Sociology of Knowledge Analysis.* New York: Longman, 1979.

Orwell, George. *1984.* 1950. New York: Signet-Penguin, 1977.

Ovid. *Metamorphoses.* Trans. Rolfe Humphries. Bloomington: Indiana University Press, 1955.

White, Curtis. *The Middle Mind: Why Americans Don't Think for Themselves.* New York: Harper Collins, 2003.

Whitman, Walt. "Song of Myself" *Walt Whitman: Complete Poetry and Selected Prose and Letters.* Ed. Emory Holloway. London: The Nonesuch Press, 1967. 84.

The Temporary Resident

Joel H. Siegel

> Just as a person resides in the
> world he or she hopes to
> understand, a reader resides,
> temporarily, in the text he or she reads.
> —John P. Niles

> No man may know wisdom till
> many a winter has been his portion.
> —Anonymous, "The Wanderer"

I note with some interest that the title of this festschrift is *wintering* into wisdom, not *wintered* into wisdom, suggesting not some product, something achieved and finished, but rather a process, something in progress, something which is ongoing. Wisdom, I take it, has to do with understanding who and what we are in relation to our world, and we never come to a complete understanding of ourselves and our world. That is an ongoing task.

We have a basic need to live a life of meaning, to feel that we matter in the universe. Perhaps, it has been suggested, that need derives from some basic dread that life, after all, is without meaning and that our lives really are inconsequential; in the vastness of time and space, we are but an eye-blink. Just as nature abhors a vacuum, we abhor the prospect that life is meaningless, that our lives are simply a random succession of moments ending in casual extinction, and that our lives ultimately count for nothing in the grand sweep of things.

We need to have meaning; we need to matter. And the meaning and the mattering is never settled. We are, as it were, under a compulsion to seek meaning, to find order and significance in our world, to look for values to live by at every stage in our lives.

———→•←———

Early on I became a reader, fascinated by language and story, and understandably I came to associate much of what I was thinking about with what I was reading. As a young undergraduate and graduate student, seeking a vocation, concerned mightily with who I was and with what role I would play in the larger world, I came under the spell of James Joyce's works, particularly *A Portrait of the Artist as a Young Man* and *Ulysses*. I identified at the time with young Stephen Dedalus in *Portrait* as he set about to forge his identity amidst the squalor and clamor of his surroundings; proud and defiant, Stephen felt his family, nation, and religion were all nets flung at his soul to keep it from flight and that he would fly by those nets. Stephen's cry was "*non serviam* I will not serve" (141)—echoing the very cry of Lucifer—the cry of one who will not serve that which he can no longer believe in, the cry of the proud rebel who will not yield to the conventional but who will defiantly and stubbornly seek his own truths and make his own path. Stephen as the quintessential rebel and quester—how that appealed to me! At one point in *Portrait*, Stephen openly rejects the priesthood and elects to be an artist, a writer—in this vocation he will be a "priest of the eternal imagination" (249), and idealistically he will seek the truth of our lives and reveal those truths to us through his art; through his art he wishes to create "the uncreated conscience" (282) of his race. Apart from the crowd, idealist, seeker after life's truths, reformer, zealous follower of a vocation—these were the attributes that I admired in Stephen. As I look back on *Portrait*, however, the single image that most stands out in my mind is the image of young Stephen writing in the flyleaf of his geography text:

Stephen Dedalus
Class of elements
Clongowes Wood College
Sallins
County Kildare
Ireland
Europe
The World
The Universe (34)

The image is emblematic of our most basic task—finding out how and where we fit in our universe.

During the time I was first reading Joyce, some 50 years ago, I came upon my vocation—teaching. At one point in my career, I regularly taught the heroic literature of early Greece, Rome, and England and came to fancy that course. I read various critics and commentators in developing my views on the period and the individual works, none to me more insightful than the brilliant work on nature and culture in the *Iliad* by James M. Redfield, to whom I am indebted for much of what follows. Heroic literature often comes to grips with the most basic facts of our existence, the fundamental nature of our being. One such passage occurs in the *Iliad* when the warrior Glaucus replies to a query about his name and lineage:

Why ask my birth, Domêdês? Very like leaves upon this
earth are the generations of men—old leaves cast on
the ground by wind, young leaves the greening forest
bears when spring comes in. So mortals pass; one
generation flowers even as another dies away. (140)

This is a stark recognition that we humans are undifferentiated in nature, that we are simply another instance of a natural process, of a natural force. Like a droplet of water or a grain of sand, in nature we are momentary and undistinguishable, ephemeral and inconsequential. But Glaucus does not stop there; he does give his name and goes on at length to detail his lineage and the community from which he comes and ends the passage expressing his determination to be among the first and foremost of the heroes. Kinship and community, then, are emphasized in the latter part of Glaucus' speech, and, as Redfield points out, kinship and community together constitute the totality of human culture (102). And it is through culture that we have names, relationships, identities, and values. It is through the human-derived institutions of government, law, and religion and through the cultural avenues of language, ceremony, ritual, and tradition that we experience the world. We may be marked for oblivion in nature, but human culture makes available to us vast resources (and the only resources) for establishing an identity and for imposing meaning on the stubborn stuff of life.

Much of what Homer put in the mouths of Glaucus and other heroes some three thousand years ago fits well with certain strands of modern thought, particularly some strains of existentialist thinking. In the works of Sartre and Camus, we get a picture of man born naked and vulnerable into an immense, indifferent universe where there are no essential directions about how to live in the brief time and space allotted us. At our birth there are no instructions in the package on how to assemble and use the life contained therein, and there are no warranties or guarantees provided. No pre-set purpose, principle, or "one size fits all" meaning of existence lies out there waiting to be uncovered. Whatever meanings or values there are in life are the ones that we bring into existence in our human culture. The American philosopher Richard Rorty expresses aptly this notion "that finite, mortal, contingently existing human beings . . . derive the meanings of their lives from . . . other finite, mortal, contingently existing human beings" (45). The Sartrean view is that we derive meaning and values through our choices, our decisions in everyday living. Further, we are free to make whatever choices we will—the only limitation on our freedom of choice is that we are NOT free NOT to choose. We must choose. And our choices are consequential, since our choices result in acts and behavior that ultimately become who and what we are; in short, choice becomes character. The exercise of a choice has a further consequence—it puts that value into the world. The male speaker in Matthew Arnold's "Dover Beach" laments to his female auditor that the world has "neither joy, nor love, nor light, nor . . . peace, nor help for pain"; then he beseeches her, "Ah, love, let us be true to one another" (166). The only possibility of love or joy or any of the other virtues or values that we crave lies in our power to create them with "one another." We admire the ancient Negress Phoenix Jackson in Eudora Welty's "A Worn Path" as she makes the repeated perilous journey to procure life-saving medicine for her grandson; through her self-sacrificing, salvational act, she imbues the world of the story with the virtue of charitableness of one human being towards another human being. In living the virtue, she creates the virtue. Over and over again, in literature and in life, we see man cast into an indifferent universe where his purpose or meaning is nowhere written but through his choices and acts, which create meaning and values and, for the most part, make the earth a fit human habitation.

I need to address two matters here briefly before moving on to my conclusion. The first is that the view elaborated above does not claim that meaning and values do not exist in our world, only that there are none apart from the individual's participation in and creation of them. The second is that the view elaborated above does not seem bleak or harsh; rather, I think, it dignifies and ennobles man by placing on him the responsibility for making meaning and creating values and invests him with the capacity to do so. Remarking on the Homeric hero, Redfield asserts that "there is a nobility in men's capacity to act and at the same time comprehend themselves and their situation" (101-02).

Margrethe: And when all our eyes
are closed, when even the ghosts
have gone, what will be left of our
beloved world? Our ruined and
dishonoured and beloved world?

Heisenberg: But in the meanwhile, in this most precious
meanwhile, there it is.

—Michael Frayn, *Copenhagen*

Andrew Marvell's poem "To His Coy Mistress" begins with "Had we but world enough and time" (32). Actually, this is all that we do have—a moment of time and a bit of space. And time, which we complain that we never have enough of, seems one of our chief preoccupations. Rushing down a hall and stopped by a colleague for a quick chat, a character in a Joseph Heller novel snaps that he doesn't have time; the colleague replies that all we have is time—what we don't have is what to do with it. What to do with it? Each day dawns a fresh day wherein the world awaits our choices and our acts. And that day, albeit a brief page in the world's history, will bear to some degree the imprint of our choices. We have a vast array of choices, ranging from the scurrilous to the saintly, from the beastly to the beatific. There are numerous voices out there urging us to make this or that choice and to behave this way or that. I wish to turn now to two voices I believe worth listening to. William Faulkner, in his Nobel Prize speech, affirms his belief that man "will not merely endure; he will prevail" (120). Man, he continues, "has a soul, a spirit capable of compassion and sacrifice and endurance" (120). Faulkner concludes his speech urging a coming generation of writers to consider the ancient verities and to remind man "of the courage and honor and hope and pride and compassion and pity and sacrifice which have been the glory of his past" (120). Some years ago in a brief essay the eminent British philosopher Bertrand Russell named the three passions that had governed his life: "the longing for love, the search for knowledge, and unbearable pity for the suffering of mankind" (17). Russell speaks of knowledge, of wishing "to understand the hearts of men and to know why the stars shine" (17). Of love, he speaks of the ecstasy and of the solace it offers in life. He sees the pain and suffering of other human beings and longs "to alleviate the evil, but I cannot, and I too suffer" (17). Both Faulkner and Russell speak to us of living in the world passionately and compassionately through exercise of head and heart. Noble choices are available.

And so, ushered into the world of time and space, living at the nexus of nature and culture, forging his way by dint of head and heart—here stands man "in the meanwhile, in this most precious meanwhile," really, it seems to me, quite the marvel of the universe.

Works Cited

Arnold, Matthew. "Dover Beach." *The Portable Matthew Arnold*. Ed. Lionel Trilling. 1949. New York: Viking, 1965. 166.

Faulkner, William. *Essays, Speeches, and Public Letters*. Ed. James B. Meriweather. New York: Random House, 2004.

Homer. *The Iliad*. Trans. Robert Fitzgerald. 1975 ed. New York: Farrar, Straus, and Giroux, 2004.

Joyce, James. *A Portrait of the Artist as a Young Man*. Eds. Hans Walter Gabler and Walter Hettche. New York: Garland, 1993.

---. *Ulysses*. New York: Random House, 1961.

Marvell, Andrew. "To His Coy Mistress." *The Complete Poems*. 1972. New York: Penguin, 1996. 32.

Redfield, James M. *Nature and Culture in the* Iliad: *The Tragedy of Hector.* Durham: Duke UP, 1994.

Rorty, Richard. *Contingency, Irony, and Solidarity.* Cambridge: Cambridge UP, 1999.

Russell, Bertrand. *The Autobiography of Bertrand Russell.* 1967 ed. New York: Routledge, 2000.

"The Wanderer." *Old English Elegies.* Ed. Charles W Kennedy. Princeton: Princeton UP, 1939. 43-52.

Welty, Eudora. "A Worn Path." *The Collected Stories of Eudora Welty.* Orlando: Harcourt, 1994. 142-152.

Nostalgia and Renewal: The Role of the College President in Shaping Campus Culture

Michael J. Siegel

> We shall not cease from exploration
> And the end of all our exploring
> Will be to arrive where we started
> And know the place for the first time
> —T.S. Eliot

Institutions of higher education are fundamentally culture-bearing organizations. That is, much of what people do on college campuses relates to discovering, understanding, and making sense of norms, values, beliefs, traditions, and other elements of culture that exist in the environment. Both in form (the physical) and in function (the behavioral), college campuses are citadels of culture. Whether one is peering inward to study the college environment from the position of lay ethnographer or looking outward from the position of native academician, a cultural lens is perhaps the most useful in describing the complexities of organizational functioning. In this essay, I make the case that colleges and universities are cultural arenas where inhabitants—for our purposes here, college presidents—invoke cultural properties such as norms, values, beliefs, artifacts, sagas, and the like to make sense of the environment. Further, I point to ways in which culture is paradoxical in that it both illuminates and limits our thinking in the academy. Finally, I discuss implications of campus culture for presidential leadership and outline ways in which college and university presidents can harness properties of campus culture to effect change.

The College as Cultural Arena

Examining college environments from a cultural frame of reference suggests using an interpretive rather than rationalistic-scientific approach to understanding campus behaviors. This interpretive view suggests that each of us in the academy helps create and sustain belief systems about organizational life by invoking symbols, behavioral norms, rituals, values, language, and other elements of culture which govern and influence the way members operate within the environment. Essentially, we construct and try to make sense of our own realities while at the same time we try to interpret the meaning that other individuals impute to the cultural environment.

In their book, *Collegiate Cultures*, Ellen Chaffee and William Tierney offer a thoughtful and apropos metaphor to describe the college environment. They liken the day-to-day experiences on a college campus to a cultural drama, whereby institutional members represent actors on a stage. They observe:

> Actors within collegiate cultures have few if any scripts to go by .... The most visible props—roles and governance arrangements—are not the ones we [members of collegiate cultures] tend to bump into. Rather, we most often trip over perceptions and attitudes, the intangibles that escape our attention even as they make up the fabric of daily organizational life. (3)

Fundamental to discovering the culture of an organization is understanding the meaning that is assigned to its cultural components, as symbolic and as layered as they might be. Of the many definitions of the concept of culture and its application to organizational behavior, one theme tends to be dominant. It is that culture—at least in the traditional anthropological sense—consists of shared values, beliefs, and behaviors that are socially acquired and used by organizational members as a shared frame of reference for understanding and measuring their own and others' behavior. It is important to note, however, that in any organizational setting there are multiple cultural realities that are represented by multiple constituencies. To be sure, it is problematic to assume that values, beliefs, and behaviors are shared by all members in the same manner. But for the sake of argument let us assume there are some elements of culture that when commonly experienced bind its inhabitants to one another in some fashion.

One of the central concerns in the study of academic culture is the way in which individuals make sense of their new environment. Given the complexity of organizational culture, sensemaking is challenging for individuals at all levels of institutional functioning. The dynamic interplay of cultural properties within any college or university context often makes it problematic for institutional members to understand the nuances of campus culture and make sense of organizational behavior. What they may not realize is that the failure to understand campus culture is often the result of too many competing interpretations and explanations, rather than too few. To be sure, institutional members often suffer from having too much information rather than too little.

Cultural properties in organizations are not only complex; they are also dynamic. Most elements of culture—for instance, strongly-held traditions, artifacts and architecture, deeply embedded values, norms of behavior, myth-like stories and sagas—are ascribed with symbolic properties. While some seem liquid-like or fluid in nature and transform as a function of changing populations in the workplace, others appear to be more frozen, or congealed, in the ethos of institutional functioning. This is to say the patterns and processes of institutional culture are stored in the people who reside and operate within the institutional environment. As positions, and people within those positions, change, so does culture.

The Perils of Habit and Routine:
When Culture Rewards Complacency

Culture is at once both a liberating and confining concept. While cultural norms, values, and behaviors provide a blueprint for understanding what goes on in any particular academic environment, these same properties have the potential to stymie creative thought and excuse us from developing other patterns of behavior and interactions that might otherwise foster positive change. Sagas, stories, and narratives—some of which are enlightening and instructive, some of which are destructive and toxic—become a part of the oral history of the campus over time. As a result of their being enmeshed in the fabric of the institution, they often perpetuate long-standing and deeply embedded myths and create a sort of poisonous atmosphere.

Values, beliefs, stories, sagas, norms of behavior, artifacts, and other elements in the institutional milieu indeed provide the casual observer with some tacit knowledge about the organizational culture as a whole, but we cannot assume these elements represent a shared frame of reference. To the contrary, it is probably safer to assume, given the large number of culturally distinct groups on campus, that there is no one frame of reference—or shared cultural perspective— but rather many.

A humorous metaphor for college life, and one that is telling about the nature of myth-making and the myriad ways disparate groups ascribe meaning to cultural events, is offered by the writer, P. F. Kluge. Following his return to his alma mater, Kenyon College, to serve as a visiting professor, he penned the classic book, *Alma Mater*, offering such lines as:

> I came here thinking of this college as an island, of myself as a traveler . . . . If I'm right in holding to this island image, I'd say that our students are visitors to the island: their term here is closed-ended. Whatever else they do here, they cannot stay. The faculty are natives, an anthropologically diverse collection of tribes and

individuals who live here in a variety of ways: there
are some rarely seen aboriginals who hug the interior,
cling to ancient folkways, worship old gods, and are
rumored to take heads, others who hang close to the
shoreline, trade handicraft, dive for coins tossed by
passengers off cruise ships, and wistfully gaze out to
sea, dreaming of escape. (119-20)

Those in the academy might see one or two of their colleagues
in Kluge's cast of characters. Among them, there are the miscreants
and larger-than-life rogue faculty members who remain fixed in
their ways and somewhat frozen in time and space. Then there are
those who ponder their sentence on the island prison as they sit and
nostalgically reminisce about a better time and place.

As the remarkable leader whom this festschrift honors is fond of
saying, "Sometimes we in the academy remember a time that never
was, and we don't want it to change." In moments of inner reflection
about our own lives in academe, or in conversations we have had with
colleagues across the hall or in public spaces, many of us, faculty
and administrators alike, have convened to lament the current state
of affairs and sentimentally ponder a golden era when dry-witted
professors roamed bucolic campus grounds and students revered
the scholarly guild. As we reconstruct and rearticulate the faded
organizational past, nostalgia acts as an opiate to anesthetize the
pain of our current predicament. To be sure, the very act of invoking
stories, sagas, and other campus myths comforts us on such occasions
and lets us retrospectively reconstruct a more exalted and majestic
institutional past.

Perhaps these images, locked and fixed in time as they are, keep
us from embracing change, adopting some new idea or cultural
shift, or—to extend the island metaphor—finally take leave of the
island putting our cultural dinghies out to sea in search of better
academic shores. In short, we see things as they once were or should
be in the future, but we fail to remember the reality of our own
present situation. As it were, such fixations keep us from renewing

ourselves and rejuvenating our sometimes ancient and archaic folkways and beliefs.

Many individuals within the university seem hesitant to promote programs and policies that risk upsetting the status quo in their departments. In short, people do not want to be seen as "getting ahead" or engaging in work or tasks that might foster resentment from their colleagues. They prefer, instead, to run in the middle of the pack, keep in step with their coworkers, and not shine too brightly in the offing. They, in short, have struck an implicit bargain with their coworkers to not ask too much from one another. Is it any wonder why change moves slowly in academe? Universities often move forward slowly in terms of changes to the curriculum, physical infrastructure, campus programming, and other areas. And if status-quo behavior is evident at one level of organizational functioning, there is likely the same behavior at other levels both below and above.

Culture and Implications for Presidential Leadership

The president's role in organizational functioning is the most important and influential to any college or university. It follows that the demands and expectations of the college community for a president are elevated to a higher standard than is true for any other person in an institution. Similarly, attempts at understanding cultural aspects of the campus and discerning common interests, goals, and aspirations are made ambiguous by the multiple expectations various constituent groups have for a new president. This ambiguity is paradoxical in the sense that more than one plausible meaning may be ascribed to certain behaviors. And it is complex in that organizational culture is comprised of a network of behaviors, norms, and beliefs that are highly subjective, defying simple explanation and understanding.

The status of the position is such that multiple, and often competing, demands are placed on the office of the president. As the demand for a president's time and attention increases and proliferates, the scrutiny of the position intensifies. Many of the decisions made, and actions taken, during the early tenure of the presidency are seen as symbolic gestures that impart messages about the values and beliefs of the president.

Impossible Expectations

Many college presidents will tell you that sometime in the early days and months of their tenure they were asked to share their "vision" for the future of the college. Ironically, the vast majority of new presidents come from outside, as opposed to inside, the institution to which they have just been selected to serve, and they do not yet have the store of knowledge about campus culture that would allow them to make such pronouncements. It follows that effective leaders of colleges and universities, particularly new presidents, must quickly become acclimated to the campus culture and serve as a catalyst through which cultural processes are understood and interpreted. Whether they serve as architects of cultural change or as spokespersons and articulators of change, they are expected to communicate institutional values in order to facilitate effective institutional functioning. As a college president once told me, "[...] presidents are supposed to be professorial and filled with wisdom and understanding."

The President as Living Logo

A classic meditation by Clifford Geertz in his book *Local Knowledge* elucidates the symbolic and emblematic nature of the presidency, suggesting that much of the stateliness and opulence that punctuates the offices of leaders gives meaning to the culture and the world in which people live. He notes that leaders

> justify their existence and order their actions
> in terms of a collection of stories, ceremonies,
> insignia, formalities, and appurtenances [trappings,
> accessories] that they have either inherited or,

in more revolutionary situations, invented. It is
these—crowns and coronations, limousines and
conferences—that mark the center as center and
give what goes in there its aura of being not merely
important but in some odd fashion connected with
the way the world is built. (124)

Symbolism in the presidency is unquestionably important, and
its influence is unmistakable. Presidents often talk about symbolism
in the role, noting daily occasions where they invoke cultural
customs and address issues related to the beliefs, values, and norms
of the institution. The Office of the President is itself inherently
symbolic, and campus constituencies, for better or worse, play a
significant role in endowing a president with symbolic properties
and ascribing symbolic meanings to his or her everyday behaviors.
Whether or not they are revered by the campus community or
perceived as generally being effective, presidents are simply the
living logos of the institution.

Practically every event on the campus in which the president is in
attendance can be construed as symbolic by institutional members.
Whether attending faculty or committee meetings, attending a
campus function or athletic event, speaking to a student group,
initiating a town hall discussion, or participating in ceremonies such
as graduation or convocation, presidents know their daily interactions
in the campus environment are replete with symbolic gestures. By the
very nature of their public persona and the multitude of occasions
where they are asked to say a few words, individuals in the campus
community "hang on every word of the president when they speak,"
as a president once told me. To that end, presidents use public
appearances and announcements as a way of sending messages to the
community, both directly and symbolically. People listen more closely
when presidents speak than when other members of the academic
community do, and they pay close attention to what presidents do
as well as to what they do not do. Behaviors and everyday activities
that might be considered routine and customary for most members

of a campus community are ascribed with highly symbolic attributes where the role of the president is concerned.

Presidents must recognize the importance of being aware of how internal and external constituents view their actions, interpret their interactions with people on and off campus, and conduct the business of the college. In that vein, presidents should learn to harness and reflect the symbolic nature of physical properties on campus as well as the behavioral. Campus artifacts such as buildings, statues, stadiums, landscaped areas, student unions, classrooms, entryways, and walking paths convey symbolic messages merely by their presence on campus.

The complexities of culture on a college campus do not unfold quickly or completely. Often elements of culture become manifest when individuals discuss with the president stories about the institution and historical events that have occurred on the campus, or enlighten the president to the various norms of behavior that have historically been rewarded and accepted on campus. In addition, values can also become exposed when individuals in the campus community react to changes that are either taking place or pending on campus, or if they perceive a new policy, program, or procedure is a threat to the current mode of operation and administration on campus. In any event, presidents learn elements of campus culture in a number of ways, sometimes discovering it through intentional behaviors and at other times "bumping into" culture when it is exposed by certain actions or triggering events on campus.

W(h)ither our Academic Giants?

In thinking about nostalgia and the role it plays in shaping both my current and past views of the academy, I am often inclined to memorialize academic heroes and giants who shaped the academy in their own inimitable way. When I "wistfully gaze out to sea," as it were, I think of a time when college and university presidents loomed larger than life in the campus environment, made grand public statements and pronouncements, and effected sweeping and swift changes to the campus culture. When I think about such academic giants, I call to mind Herman B. Wells, the legendary and charismatic president of Indiana University from 1937–1962, who is widely considered to be one of the most important higher education leaders of the twentieth-century. He was a beloved character and a person of extraordinary moral fiber. He ushered in a period of unprecedented growth and change and built the school into one of the great universities of the world. As a man of vision, he was clearly ahead of his time, and as a man who understood and defined campus culture, he was without peer. He championed many causes, some of them popular and some of them unpopular, and he was willing to stand alone in support of what he knew was right and just.

Many people are familiar with Wells' leadership during the storm of controversy that surrounded the university in the 1950s with respect to the work of Dr. Alfred Kinsey, the noted professor and sex researcher who collected thousands of sex histories for the purposes of research. In what many consider to be one of the landmark victories for academic freedom, Wells supported Kinsey and protected the Kinsey Institute for Sex Research from being dismantled. Wells remarked in his memoir years later,

> For me, there was really no question about support of
> Kinsey's research. I had early made up my mind that a
> university that bows to the wishes of a person, group, or
> segment of society is not free and that a state university
> in particular cannot expect to command the support of
> the public if it is captive to any group. (179)

Less is known about Wells' initiatives to address discrimination on campus. One particular incident is related to the use of campus facilities by black students, specifically the discrimination of black students from using the men's swimming pool. Wells was clever in his determination, as witnessed by a particularly fascinating story that found him arranging for the pool to be integrated. Calling on the athletic director, he asked when the pool was most heavily used.

He then asked who the most popular black athlete was on campus, whom he soon learned was a certain Rooster Coffee, a football player. Wells said, "Some afternoon next week when the pool is quite full, go down on the floor, find Rooster, and tell him to strip in the locker room and go jump in the pool" (217). Incredulous, the athletic director asked if Wells meant it. "Yes," Wells replied, "and don't tell anybody, even Rooster, what you're going to do in advance" (217). The story goes that the athletic director spoke one day with Rooster, who then stripped, jumped in the pool, swam, as Wells said, "with abandon for a half hour or so" (217). In his memoir, Wells recounts, "He was so cordially greeted, I doubt that anyone realized a policy had been changed. That was the last of discrimination against blacks in the use of the pool" (217).

Presidents such as Herman Wells figured prominently in the collective academic psyche of the time, having waded into debate after debate and fiercely protected the interests of the academy. There was a time when presidents took stands on issues and risked their reputations and that of their institutions to stand up for what was right and good. Presidential tenure during such a time period was indeed longer, perhaps both because and in spite of their willingness to get involved in national discussions and speak on behalf of the academic intelligentsia. As the cultural drama of campus life unfolded in academe during this golden age, presidents like Wells seemed to capture and reflect the tenets of institutional culture through various means, including improvisation, experimentation, and inventiveness.

Presidents are more likely than ever before to make the news because of questionable ethical conduct that has legal, moral, and financial implications for an institution. With our collective tongues firmly planted in our respective cheeks, we can ironically say that presidents' salaries around the country are rising to college coach-like proportions. College presidents have become increasingly reluctant to tackle potentially divisive and thorny issues when they witness events like the recent debacle at Harvard

University, in which then-president Larry Summers virtually self-destructed and brought down his own presidency with his garish and confrontational behavior and several poorly chosen remarks. What is called for now is presidential leadership from the days of old, but it is troubling to think that the days when presidents were considered first among equals, giants who were revered by educators, politicians, and citizens alike, are long gone.

Another towering presidential figure, Clark Kerr, the legendary and controversial president of the University of California System, cast a long shadow over the better part of last half-century with his leadership during a particular stormy time in the country's history. As an associate professor in the 1950s, he made a name and earned the respect of his faculty colleagues by fighting against the firing of faculty members who refused to sign anti-communist oaths that were being required of academics at the time. Ultimately named Chancellor of the University of California, Berkeley campus, in the 1950s and then later President of the University of California System, Kerr is perhaps best known as the architect of the California Master Plan for Higher Education, a three-tier system of major university campuses, state universities, and community colleges which provided extraordinary access to public higher education and left a blueprint for educational programming and system structuring in the decades that followed.

Perhaps what comes to mind for many, both inside and outside of the academy, when Clark Kerr is remembered is his leadership during the turbulent Free Speech Movement of the mid-1960s, which thrust Berkeley into the center of a national debate on the limitations of free speech and political activities on college campuses. Though the resulting conflagration fomented student activism around the country and ultimately became the undoing of Kerr's presidency, he will forever be remembered by critics and supporters alike for navigating the Berkeley campus through the Scylla of the liberal students on one side and the Charybdis of conservative politicians on the other.

Kerr was at once a product of the academy and one of its most passionate social critics, and through it all he was until the very end the "Dean" of college presidents and the first among equals in that elite group. One of higher education's most visible public intellectuals, he was also quite well know for his humor and wit and with a few choice passages could sum up and characterize the university and the office of the president in an unprecedented fashion. Consider his penetrating insight into the life of a college president in his seminal book, *The Uses of the University*:

> The university president in the United States is expected to be a friend of the students, a colleague of the faculty, a good fellow with the alumni, a sound administrator with the trustees, a good speaker with the public, an astute bargainer with the foundations and the federal agencies, a politician with the state legislature, a friend of industry, labor, and agriculture, a persuasive diplomat with the donors, a champion of education generally, a supporter of the professions (particularly law and medicine), a spokesman to the press, a scholar in his own right, a public servant at the state and national levels, a devotee of opera and football equally, a decent human being, a good husband and father, an active member of a church. Above all he must enjoy traveling in airplanes, eating his meals in public, and attending public ceremonies. No one can be all of these things. Some succeed at being none. (22)

Two statements for which he is perhaps most fondly remembered reveal his clever views on life inside the academy from the vantage point of the presidency. Both have become ensconced in the higher education lore, no doubt mythologized over the decades through countless retellings at faculty cocktail parties. The first of these comments famously made its way into both *Time* and *Playboy* magazines—not the surest sign one has arrived as a college president, but nonetheless a distinction of note reserved for a precious few in the pantheon of college presidents whose wry quips were elevated to greatness via reference in popular culture. As then-chancellor at Berkeley in 1957, Kerr was asked at a faculty meeting what he was doing about the campus parking problem. He famously replied he thought the chancellor's job had come to be characterized as "providing parking for faculty, sex for students, and athletics for alumni" (qtd. in Selingo A1). The second passage concerns his leaving the presidency. Though he was fired from the UC System after the unrest at Berkeley and later became Chairman of the Carnegie Commission (from whose helm he championed many federal policy issues), he often joked about the painful event. Of particular note, he was fond of telling people that he left the California presidency the way that he entered it, "…fired with enthusiasm" (qtd. in Selingo A1).

These two presidential giants served during a time when the tenure in office was marked for many leaders in decades rather than years. That famed generation of presidents was, like any other, a product of its own time and place—the intersection where personal biography meets history. They were perhaps no more or less principled than today's college presidents and no more or less concerned with the academy's position, role, and responsibility in the greater sphere of social life. We do know the ivory tower was at that time less permeable by outside forces, and therefore less subject to the multiple winds of environmental change that act as pressure points on today's college presidencies. Perhaps the vaunted office of the president was more treasured, respected, and revered in the middle of the past century than it is at the beginning of this one. Perhaps they were better able to use their positions of power and influence to move the needle of change towards more effective national educational policymaking, essentially keeping the academy at the center of national conversation on large-scale social issues. Whether or not the relatively short term of today's average presidency is the result of too much meddling in controversial matters or not enough is a matter best left for pundits, politicians, and Monday-morning armchair quarterbacks.

The President as Culture Manager: Final Reflections

With increasing pressure from external constituents, demands for new leadership paradigms, growing fiscal concerns in many state systems of education, and changing patterns in the nature of faculty tenure, campus leaders continue to face significant challenges. I have attempted in this brief essay to convey the importance of engaging in cultural sensemaking as a means for college and university presidents to govern more effectively and make significant changes in our so-called arenas of campus culture. Among the most important objectives for any president are to discover and understand the various nuances and levels of organizational culture. In order to function effectively, presidents must broadly consider the needs and concerns of a vast array of constituent groups, both internal and external to the campus, when carrying out their official duties. They must be able to transcend the boundaries that set apart various campus subcultures, and they should be adroit at bringing together campus groups that often have disparate values and beliefs. In short, they must be boundary spanners. They must find ways to utilize components of culture to communicate ideas and effect change on campus.

To change campus culture, presidents are best served knowing they have multiple options to employ and several levels at which they may proceed. They must determine whether a campus needs to be radically transformed, changed moderately, or simply managed and maintained in its current status. The extent to which change is needed, desired, or both, has to be considered by presidents when programming and planning. Traditionally, many individuals and constituency groups have to be consulted before culture-changing initiatives are put into motion.

Presidents should consider themselves change managers as well as change makers. They should anticipate the potential disruption to campus culture when they enact policies or initiatives that "bump up against" strong traditions, widely held beliefs, core values, and norms of behavior that have become part of the ethos of an institution.

Presidents learn their role most effectively when they intentionally attempt to understand, respect, and utilize core institutional values.

It is not enough for a president to explore culture and learn how to strategically operate within a campus environment. He or she must be able to convey respect and an appreciation for the core values and traditions of a college or university. The deeper one's understanding of the levels at which culture exists, the more effective the president will be at governing with the best interests of the college or university stakeholders in mind. It is not possible for presidents to discover and understand all of the nuances of their institution's culture. There are no blueprints or templates for reaching a deep understanding of culture in institutions of higher education. This is not to suggest that institutional culture is a random and loosely coupled array of behaviors, interactions, beliefs, and philosophies at work in an organizational environment. It is to say, rather, that there is no one best way to discover the key elements of an institution's culture that drive institutional behavior and functioning. If we assume there are no universally accepted and fixed notions of culture that drive the daily operation of organizational environments, then we cannot expect presidents to fully understand the tenets of organizational culture.

Of the many architects of campus culture, presidents have the greatest responsibility of any institutional member to discover, interpret, and ultimately manage campus culture. It is not surprising that presidents have had, and continue to have, the most significant impact on colleges or universities of anyone in the college community, however real or perceived that influence might be. Whether they bring to their position a blueprint for understanding culture, or whether they are in search of one that may or may not already exist, presidents routinely search for the most effective ways to manage and direct the unfolding drama of campus culture. Perhaps this is their most significant contribution to the academy.

To meet the challenges of the office, presidents must be informed and knowledgeable about campus culture, and beyond that they must be skillful in utilizing cultural elements when carrying out their official duties as president. Presidents are bestowed with an enormous amount of power and influence when they assume their role. With that power and influence, presidents have a responsibility to serve as the key representative of their institutions as well as their primary culture-bearers.

Works Cited

Chaffee, Ellen Earle, and William G. Tierney. *Collegiate Culture and Leadership Strategies*. New York: MacMillan, 1988.

Geertz, Clifford. *Local Knowledge: Further Essays in Interpretive Anthropology*. New York: Basic-Perseus, 1983.

Kerr, Clark. *The Uses of the University*. (4th Edition). Cambridge: Harvard University Press, 1995.

Kluge, P. F. *Alma Mater*. New York: Addison-Wesley, 1993.

Selingo, J. "Clark Kerr, 'One of the Giants,' dies." *The Chronicle of Higher Education*. 12 Dec. 2003: A1. 24 Jan. 2007 <http://chronicle.com/free/v50/i16/16a00101.htm>.

Wells, Herman B. *Being Lucky*. Bloomington: Indiana UP, 1980.

Contributors

Betsy O. Barefoot is the current co-director and senior scholar for the Policy Center on the First Year of College in Brevard, NC, and a fellow of the University of South Carolina's National Resource Center for the First-Year Experience in Columbia, SC. Dr. Barefoot is co-author of *Your College Experience* (7th ed., 2006) with John N. Gardner and A. Jerome Jewler; *Achieving and Sustaining Institutional Excellence for the First College Year* (2005) with John N. Gardner, Marc Cutright, and Libby V. Morris; and *Challenging and Supporting the First-Year Students: A Handbook for Improving the First Year of College* (2005); as well as numerous other articles and books.

Betsy Downer Brown, a graduate of Kennesaw State University, teaches ninth-grade Pre-AP English and Honors British Literature at Carrolton High School in Carrolton, GA. She has served as an instructional lead teacher as well as an SAT/ACT review teacher.

Johnetta B. Cole has served as president of Bennett College for Women in Greensboro, NC (2002-06), and Spelman College in Atlanta, GA (1987-97), both historically black colleges for women. She was the Presidential Distinguished Professor of Anthropology, Women's Studies, and African American Studies at Emory University in Atlanta, and she has also taught at Hunter College of the City University of New York; Oberlin College in OH; Williams College in Williamstown, MA; the University of Massachusetts at Amherst; Washington State University; and the University of California at Los Angeles. Dr. Cole's most recent book is *Gender Talk: The Struggle for Women's Equality in African American Communities* (2003), and she serves on the editorial board for *Common Quest, Journal for Higher Education Management, The Black Scholar,* and *Souls.* She is the recipient of many awards, including the Uncommon Height Award from the National Council of Negro Women (2006), the Joseph Prize for Human Rights from the Anti-Defamation League (2004), and the Women Who Make a Difference Award from the National Council for Research on Women (2002).

Elizabeth Giddens is an associate professor of English at Kennesaw State University where she teaches writing to undergraduates and to graduate students in the Master of Arts in Professional Writing Program. Dr. Giddens has been an editor and associate communications director for the Southern Regional Education Board in Atlanta, GA, and a communications analyst and director of communications for the RAND Institute for Civil Justice in Santa Monica, CA. She is a co-author of *Class Action Dilemmas: Pursuing Public Goals for Private Gain* (2000) with Deborah R. Hensler, Nicholas M. Pace, Bonita Dombey-Moore, Jennifer Gross, and Erik K. Moller, and of *Crafting Prose* (1989) with Don R. Cox. She recently published "Qualitative Research on What Leads to Success in Professional Writing" in the *International Journal for the Scholarship of Teaching and Learning* with Margaret Walters and Susan Hunter (2007) and "Context Matters: Recognizing the Effects of Epistemic and Agonistic Contexts in Public Policy Debate" in *Issues in Writing* (2006).

Sally Z. Hare is president of still learning, inc. in Surfside Beach, SC, as well as Elizabeth and Grant Singleton Distinguished Professor Emeritus and founding director of the Center for Education and Community at Coastal Carolina University in Conway, SC. She is the recipient of many awards and honors, including the Phenomenal Woman in South Carolina Award presented by *The State* newspaper (2003), the Outstanding Woman of South Carolina Award presented by the governor (2002), and an award for The Courage to Teach,

Fetzer National Pilot Program with Dr. Parker J. Palmer (1996-98). Dr. Hare has received large grants for The Southeastern Courage to Teach from the Fetzer Foundation and a private donor, and for Jump for the Sun II: A Collaborative Research Project to Encourage Girls and Women in Science and Math from the National Science Foundation. Her most recent publication is a chapter titled "*The Lehrergarten*: A Vision of Teacher Education" in *Living the Questions (2005)*, edited by Sam Intrator.

Johnny Isakson, an Atlanta native and member of the Republican Party, currently represents the State of Georgia in the U.S. Senate. He has previously served in the Georgia General Assembly (1976-90), the Georgia Senate (1993-96), and the U.S. House of Representatives (1999-2004). He has also had a successful career in real estate and served as the chair of the Georgia Board of Education in 1996.

Nancy S. King, vice president for Student Success and Enrollment at Kennesaw State University, is a consultant on freshman-year experience programs and academic advising for over 40 universities and colleges. Dr. King has long been a leader in the National Academic Advising Association (NACADA), serving on its board of directors (1987-89), as president-elect (1995-96), president (1996-97), and past president (1999-2001). She has served as the advisor to KSU's Golden Key National Honor Society chapter since it was chartered. Her awards include the first Outstanding Advisor of the Year Award from the Golden Key National Honor Society (1998), the Service to NACADA Award (2001), and a Woman of Achievement Award (2006) from the Northwest Georgia YWCA.

Joseph D. Meeks has served as dean of the College of the Arts at Kennesaw State University since 1996. Previously, he was chair of the Music Department. Dean Meeks, a pianist, has taught classes in music theory, music appreciation, piano literature and pedagogy. In

2000 he was recognized for arts leadership and named Lexus Leader of the Arts at Kennesaw State University. During the same year, he was presented with an Abbey Award, which is a Coca Cola Lifetime Achievement Award for Arts Leadership.

William Watson Purkey is professor emeritus of counselor education at the University of North Carolina at Greensboro and a co-founder of the International Alliance for Invitational Education. Dr. Purkey is the recipient of the University of North Carolina System's The Board of Governors' Award for Excellence in Teaching, and the Royal Conservatory of Music's 2005 Excellence in Education Award. He is co-author of *Becoming an Invitational Leader* (2002) with Dr. Betty Siegel, and of *Positive Discipline: A Pocketful of Ideas* (1986) with David B. Strahan. In 2006 he published *Teaching Class Clowns (and What They Can Teach Us)*.

Ferrol Sams, is a physician, humorist, and novelist, renown for his trilogy about Porter Osborne, Jr., a hero whose life mirrors Sams' own childhood in Fayette County, GA. The trilogy includes *Run with the Horseman* (1982), a national best seller; *The Whisper of the River* (1984); and *When All the World Was Young* (1991), which won the Townsend Prize for Fiction. Dr. Sams is a graduate of Mercer University in Macon, GA, and of Emory University School of Medicine in Atlanta. Since 1951, Dr. Sams has practiced medicine with his wife, Helen Fletcher, also a physician, in Fayetteville, GA, where they established the Fayette Medical Center in 1987. He has taught creative writing at Emory University and medical classes at Emory Medical School. In 2006 *Run with the Horsemen* was selected as the inaugural text in the Atlanta Reads: One Book, One Community program.

Howard Shealy teaches history at Kennesaw State University and serves as chair of the Department of History and Philosophy.

From 1996 to 2001 he served as assistant dean in the College of Humanities and Social Sciences. Dr. Shealy is the director of the university's Montepulciano, Italy, study-abroad program, and in 1991 he won the KSU Distinguished Teaching Award.

David J. Siegel is an associate professor in the Department of Educational Leadership at East Carolina University in Greenville, NC, where he teaches courses in organizational theory and culture, qualitative research in education, and policy analysis and development. Dr. Siegel has several articles in press for various journals, including *The Journal of Higher Education*, and the *International Journal of Educational Advancement*. He is also the author of *The Call for Diversity: Pressure, Expectation, and Organizational Response in the Postsecondary Setting* (2005). He serves on the Diversity Committee for the College of Education at ECU and is a member of the European Association of Institutional Research.

Joel H. Siegel, is a professor of English, a lawyer, and a municipal judge. He has taught courses in Old English, English literature, English composition, history of the English language, linguistics, and business law at the University of Florida; Edinburgh University in Scotland; Western Carolina University in Cullowhee, NC; Spelman College in Atlanta, GA; Dalton College, GA; and Piedmont College, GA. He is an associate judge at the City of Kennesaw Municipal Court and has practiced law with Brock and Clay in Marietta, GA, and Cohn, Turpin & Walker in Woodstock, GA. Since 1987, his legal concentration has been real estate law, and he currently has a solo practice. Dr. Siegel is an honorary commander of the Cobb Chamber of Commerce in Cobb County, GA, and he does community service work with many organizations in Cobb County, including the Kiwanis Club, the WellStar Hospital Hospice Committee, The Cobb County Landmark Society, the Cobb-Marietta Girls Club, the Theater-in-the-Square, and the Cobb Chapter of the American Cancer Society.

Michael J. Siegel is an assistant professor and director for the Administration of Higher Education Program at Suffolk University in Boston, MA, where he teaches courses in organization, research methods, and leadership. He is an associate consultant for Noel-Levitz, a nationally recognized consulting firm specializing in higher education student recruitment, financial aid, student retention, market research and Web and communications development. In addition, Dr. Siegel has been a fellow of the Policy Center on the First Year of College in Brevard, NC, from 2001-04. He is author of *Primer on Assessment of the First College Year* (2003) and co-author of *Service-learning Across Cultures: Promise and Achievement (2004)* and of *Achieving and Sustaining Institutional Excellence for the First Year of College (2005)*.

Printed in the United States
140951LV00002B/4/A